THE TOP CYCLISTS

Peloton Legends

OF THE MODERN ERA

By Eric Bowen

2020 Printing

ISBN : 979-8-6425-4510-2

Thank You

There is absolutely no way I could have completed this book without help and support of all the following:

My family – Kathy, Paige (for her wonderful cover/jacket concept), Shaun, Gwen, Emalie and my mother, Sandy. I love you all. Thanks for putting up with me for so long, especially for the last couple years while this book became reality and so much of my time was devoted to its completion.

Rob Peugh, for his wonderful design expertise. What you are holding in your hands is the fruit of all his hard work in bringing this book to life over the last year. You can find him at *www.thinkdeepcreative.com*

Amy, for all her editing help and feedback, friendship and support, and for providing the blueprint for all the Scoring Sheets.

All my former co-workers at Revolution Bike Shop in Solana Beach, CA – Joel (owner of the shop), Dano (owner of the service department), Mikki, Stephen, Noah, Brent, Brian, Howard, and Blue. Sorry you had to listen to me blather on about this project for so long.

All my Cyclopaths riding buddies and friends. Our Spain, Italy, and Big Bear trips will always be something I cherish (even when I got stranded in Italy with my dear friend Annie).

Faton, for his help with editing, providing valuable feedback, and friendship.

Su, for helping to correct the many "gremlins" after the initial publication.

Rachel Petruccillo, for the awesome illustrations found at the beginning of Parts I-V and on page 75 and 286. Her work can be found on prints, coffee mugs, t-shirts, and stickers at the CyclingArtStudio at the Etsy website.

Cor Vos and his wonderful wife Carla, for the use of his amazing photos found throughout the book.

The team at Alamy, for helping me acquire picture rights to many of the hard to find archival photos.

All the contributors of their photography who have shared their work with the world via Wiki Commons. A complete list of all photo and illustration credits can be found at the end of the book.

Contents

Preface

PELOTON LEGENDS

Back in 2008 I created a road cycling blog called The Virtual Musette (now defunct). As I was looking for ideas for a new article, I stumbled across a cycling fan forum debating which professional male cyclist was the greatest in the history of the sport. It became abundantly clear that aside from Eddy Merckx and Lance Armstrong, many fans of the sport were sadly unaware of the other great cyclists whose names should come up when discussing the legends of the sport. Thus, was born the inspiration for creating the ranking system now known as *Peloton Legends: The Top 100 Cyclists of the Modern Era*.

So, how does one begin to determine which professional cyclists were the best of the best? For starters, how do you even begin to compare riders who competed at different times and who never competed against each other? Also, how do you compare some of the all-time greats who had completely different types of *palmarès* (career victories)? As a prime example of two such cyclists, consider Miguel Induráin and Roger De Vlaeminck, the former a Grand Tour

Miguel Induráin

specialist who competed in the 1980s and 1990s, and the latter a Classics specialist who competed in the 1970s.

Most cycling fans are aware that Miguel Induráin's legacy in the sport was secured by becoming the first cyclist to capture five consecutive wins in the most prominent race on the calendar, the Tour de France. "Big Mig's" name will forever be linked to *La Grande Boucle* (The Big Loop). Yet, despite Induráin's incredible run of victories in the Tour, it must also be noted that his lifetime victory count does not include even one of cycling's premier single-day races, the Monuments. These are the most prestigious Classics on the calendar—Milan-San Remo, the Tour of Flanders, Paris-Roubaix, Liège-Bastogne-Liège, and Il Lombardia.

Far less well known, especially among many American fans, are the accomplishments of Roger De Vlaeminck. His track record in

Roger De Vlaeminck

one-day races is simply one of the best in the history of the sport. "Mr. Paris-Roubaix" not only captured the famed cobbled Classic four times, but more significantly, he is one of only three cyclists to have won all five of the Monuments (along with Eddy Merckx and Rik Van Looy). Consider this: Only three cyclists achieved this amazing Monument sweep, as compared to four cyclists who were able to win the Tour de France five times—Jacques Anquetil, Merckx, Bernard Hinault, and Induráin (five, if we include Lance Armstrong's stripped victories).

So, which is the greater accomplishment, capturing all five Monuments or winning the Tour five times? Yet, as impressive as his results in the Monuments may be, De Vlaeminck's winning ways didn't carry over into Miguel Induráin's forte, the Tour de France. Although De Vlaeminck entered the race three times, he never once managed to finish it. Although he did win one stage in the Tour, it's an odd and striking contrast to his four points classifications and twenty-two stage victories in Italy's Grand Tour, the Giro d'Italia.

Indeed, Induráin and De Vlaeminck represent pro cycling's yin and yang, each with overwhelming, dominating success in one type of racing, contrasted with very little in another, yet both cyclists are considered among the greatest in the sport. Again, how can one possibly compare riders with such different talents and careers, an analysis further complicated when the two competed in different eras? Ultimately, what is the proper place for both athletes in the pecking order of all-time greats?

Peloton Legends is the ranking system I've created to answer those questions. Points have been assigned to all male* professional cyclists who competed in the modern era (1935–present). In the following sections I'll discuss the problems inherent in developing such a system; why I chose to exclude earlier time periods; which races were included, and the point values assigned to each; the adjustment formulas that were used to recognize special lifetime accomplishments; and lastly, each cyclist's ranking along with their point totals.

I'm sure there will be fans of certain cyclists who won't agree with the final rankings, but the final order of cyclists was never really the entire intended purpose. The true goal of *Peloton Legends* was to provide cycling fans with a deeper appreciation for the sport's rich history and serve as a primer for some of its greatest riders—giants of the road who are often overlooked when discussing "the best cyclists ever." I hope to have played some small part in furthering that objective (if you'd like to know more about the author, please visit PelotonLegends.com).

---

* *Female cyclists are addressed in the Epilogue on page 277.*

Ruhl Petruccelli

Part I

COMPARING CYCLING'S
TWO MAJOR ERAS

Comparing Cycling's Two Major Eras

THE HEROIC ERA & THE MODERN ERA

OF COURSE, THERE ARE SEVERAL PROBLEMS ENCOUNTERED when
trying to put together any kind of ranking system for the best riders
of all time. Chief among these are comparing riders from different
eras; accounting for gaps in riders' careers due to war or injury; and
changes to the race calendar through the years.

As I started researching and compiling data on races and riders, it
became clear that it would be too difficult to compare cyclists from
what I will call the Heroic Era (the turn of the century to 1934) to
those of the Modern Era (1935 to the present). These cutoff dates
will make more sense considering the comparisons, and contrasts,
to follow. In the end, I think you'll agree that it is a fruitless exercise
to compare a rider from the early age of road racing, such as
Philippe Thys (the first three-time winner of the Tour de France), to
one his modern counterparts, like Chris Froome. Ultimately, these
types of comparisons become pointless given the profound
differences in the two time periods.

First off, it just wasn't that easy to get around Europe during the first
half of the twentieth century. Consequently, most riders tended to
race in their home countries. When
Italy's Fiorenzo Magni won the Tour
of Flanders in 1949, he was only the
second rider from outside Belgium to
have won the race since its inception
in 1913 (Switzerland's Henri Suter
was the first in 1923). Similar
patterns could be found at the other
Northern Classics, Liège-Bastogne-
Liège and Paris-Roubaix. Likewise,
the Italian Classics, Milan-San Remo
and the Giro di Lombardia, rarely
featured winners from outside Italy,
especially from the end of
World War I to 1950.

Philippe Thys

The Grand Tours also exhibited these
same regional biases. Prior to 1938,

there was only one Italian who managed to win the Tour de France, Ottavio Bottecchia. He accomplished this, and in consecutive years for good measure in 1924 and 1925, while riding as member of a French team.

Ottavio Bottecchia

The Giro d'Italia proved to be even more nationally exclusive than its French counterpart. Since its inception in 1909, the Italians had won every edition of their Grand Tour until Switzerland's Hugo Koblet finally broke their long string of victories in 1950. As for the Spaniards, they were almost nonexistent in any of the significant one-day races or Grand Tours prior to the end of World War II, racing almost exclusively in their homeland.

It's also important to note that many of the significant races used in this scoring system did not even exist during most of the Heroic Era. Ghent-Wevelgem wasn't introduced until 1934. La Flèche Wallonne's first run didn't occur until 1936. The Tour of Spain wasn't launched until 1935. Even the World Championship Road Race didn't exist prior to 1927. Further, all the classification competitions in the Grand Tours made their first appearances after 1932—the Tour de France's mountains classification debuted in 1933 and its points classification in 1953; the Giro d'Italia's mountains classification debuted in 1933 and its points classification in 1966.

Further complicating comparisons of the Heroic Era to the Modern Era was the emphasis on individual efforts in the early racing years versus the team tactics that played a much more prominent role in later years. The Tour even had a category for individual riders who were not part of a team. Teamwork was not fully realized until the mid-'20s, when Lucien Buysse was widely credited with being the first true domestique (the literal French translation is "servant"), sacrificing his chances at the 1925 Tour de France in order to help Ottavio Bottecchia secure his second victory.

No overview of the early days of racing would be complete without noting that World War I decimated the professional ranks, as many cyclists never returned from battle or were

Lucien Buysse

too seriously injured to ever race again. The notable names killed in action included Luxembourg's Francois Faber, the Tour winner of 1909; France's Octave Lapize, another Tour winner (1910) who also won Paris-Roubaix three consecutive times from 1909 to 1911; and also, France's Lucien "Petit-Breton," the first man to win the Tour two times in a row (1907 and 1908).

Lucien Petit Breton

The Great War also took a huge bite out of the careers of many others, including Philippe Thys, Firmin Lambot, Henri Pellisier, and the first great Italian champion, Costante Girardengo. Thys had back-to-back Tour de France victories just before the race was put on hold from 1915 to 1918, and then won again in 1920. Might he have been the first rider to win not only three Tours, but four, five, or more?

Comparing Cycling's Two Major Eras

THE HEROIC ERA AND THE TOUR DE FRANCE

COMPARING TOUR DE FRANCE CHAMPIONS from the Heroic Era to those of the Modern Era is very problematic, as the Tour was once a very different race. From the mid-1920s to the late '30s, the event eventually evolved into what most of us would now consider its modern incarnation, but those transition years, and especially the very early editions, were definitely a world apart.

From 1905–1912 the winner wasn't even determined by lowest accumulated time, but rather by a point system. Had such an arrangement been in place when he raced, would Germany's Erik Zabel (points classification winner from 1996 to 2001) possibly have been the first six-time consecutive Tour winner?

Eric Zabel

The length of the stages in the early editions of the Tour was brutal. Recent editions of the race average around 2,175 miles (3,500 km) spread over twenty-one stages. Through the mid-1920s, the race's total length was around 3,300 miles (5,500 km) spread over only fifteen stages. This meant the average stage was often a marathon day in the saddle featuring 220-plus leg-breaking miles (366 km) on bikes weighing well over thirty pounds (13.6 kg). Keep in mind, the longest of the Classics, Milan-San Remo, is "only" 180 miles (298 km) long. These extreme distances often pushed the total elapsed time for the Tour winner past two hundred hours, more than double that of recent champions. It was during this earlier era that reporter Albert Londres coined the famous term "convicts of the road" after an interview with Henri Pellisier (Tour winner in 1923) who lamented, "We are treated like beasts in a circus."

Henri Pellisier

The Tour's founder, Henri Desgrange, also enforced draconian rules which required riders to make all repairs without assistance, and until 1928 spare parts weren't even allowed. Good fortune often played as large a part in victory as did a rider's skill and endurance. Additionally, the cyclists were also required to carry everything with them, from the start of the stage until the finish, including all their clothing and spare tires; nothing could be discarded. This was no small task, as the clothing of the era was made from bulky wool, which could not be easily stored once removed.

Henri Desgrange

The early Tour winners seemed to have been cut from a different cloth than their postwar counterparts; they were as at home on the cobbles of Paris-Roubaix as on the mountain roads of the Alps and Pyrenees. In fact, fifteen of the twenty-one different Tour victors from the Heroic Era would also make their way to the podium in the Queen of the Classics. In contrast, during the Modern Era (post-1935), only seven of the twenty-four different Tour winners also wound up placing in Paris-Roubaix. One conclusion is that perhaps Tour champions may have been a bit more robustly built than their modern counterparts. It would also stand to reason these types of riders tended to excel in the longer stages and harsher road conditions imposed by the prewar Tour.

All told, the Tour de France was a far different animal from what it became, and it is difficult to say how early pioneers would have fared in recent times. Conversely, would a tiny mountain specialist, like Italy's Marco Pantani or Colombia's Nairo Quintana (both multiple Grand Tour winners), have ever been a factor in the rough and tumble early years, racing over jarring dirt tracks, war-torn roads, and unpaved alpine passes?

Marco Pantani (Above), Nairo Quintana (Below)

Comparing Cycling's Two Major Eras

COMPARING THE HEROIC ERA
TOUR DE FRANCE AND GIRO D'ITALIA

IN THE PREVIOUS SECTION I STARTED TO ILLUSTRATE why it doesn't make a lot of sense to compare the great champions who competed in the Heroic Era (pre-1935) to the champions of the Modern Era (1935–present). That said, given the differences between the Tour de France and Giro d'Italia during this earlier time period, does it even make sense to compare Heroic Era Grand Tour champions?

Alfredo Binda was perhaps the greatest champion of the Heroic Era. He won the Giro d'Italia five times (1925, 1927–1929, and 1933), which is a record he shares with two other cycling legends, Fausto Coppi and Eddy Merckx. During these five Giro victories, he captured forty-one of its stages—a record that stood for seventy years, finally broken in 2003 when Mario Cipollini won his forty-second Giro stage (his last in the race). Binda was also a three-time World Champion (a record he shares with Rik Van Steenbergen, Merckx, Óscar Freire, and Peter Sagan), was a four-time winner of the Giro di Lombardia, and a two-time winner of Milan-San Remo. Yet, despite these remarkable achievements, he never won the Tour de France. He did enter the race, but only once in 1930. Binda had to pull out of that Tour after falling far out of contention, the victim of crashes on two different stages.

In addition to Binda, other successful Italians from his era did attempt to win the Tour de France. Francesco Camusso, Antonio Pesenti, and most notably Learco Guerra had all won the Giro d'Italia. They did have some success in the Tour (all of them placed), but none managed to make it to the top step of the podium in France.

Consider the multiple Tour de France winners from Binda's time: Ottavio Bottechia, (1924 and 1925), who although Italian, rode for a French team; Nicolas Frantz (1927 and 1928); Andre Leducq (1930

and 1932); and Antonin Magne (1931 and 1934)—none of these two-time Tour winners ever stood on the podium of the Giro. In the final analysis, how can we possibly determine the best Grand Tour cyclist of this period? Was it one of the multiple Tour champions, or Binda?

Gino Bartali (Left)

All told, we are left to wonder if the Grand Tours were once so dissimilar that maybe it was just too difficult for one cyclist to win both. Perhaps Binda came to this conclusion after his misfortune at the 1930 Tour. As discussed in the last section, it was certainly a chore traveling back in those days, but that still doesn't entirely explain why no one was able to tame both Grand Tours. Whatever the reasons, there can be no doubt that it was much harder to win both the Tour and the Giro during the Heroic Era.

Throughout the 1930s the Tour de France organizers were coming under pressure to modernize the race. Many of the onerous rules established by Henri Desgrange were viewed as antiquated and were finally abolished. Finally, as the two Grand Tours shared more common ground, someone was able to master both. In 1938 Gino Bartali made history when he won the Tour de France, having already claimed the Giro d'Italia in 1936 and 1937; it's even possible he might have won both races in 1937, had he not crashed while wearing the yellow jersey in his first Tour attempt.

Learco Guerra

Henri Desgrange died in 1940, and with the passing of the Tour de France's founding father, the final page had been turned on cycling's first great era. When the Grand Tours resumed after World War II, another fifteen cyclists would eventually go on to conquer both the Giro and the Tour de France, seven of them even managing to win both races in the same year (most recently accomplished by Marco Pantani in 1998). Most of these Tour/Giro champions will appear in the final rankings.

Comparing Cycling's Two Major Eras

THE TRANSITION TO THE MODERN ERA

No discussion comparing the two major eras would be complete without addressing perhaps the greatest difference between the two: the widespread use of the rear derailleur. We take for granted the ease with which we change gears on a road bike, but it wasn't always so. Up until the mid-1930s, racing bikes typically had only two gears, one for climbing and one for descending and the flats. These gears were changed by dismounting the bike, removing the rear wheel, flipping it around to access the gear on the other side of the hub, and finally reinstalling and tightening the wheel with wing nuts. All told, a rather onerous procedure and certainly not the most effective way of launching a surprise attack in an uphill effort. The rear derailleur changed all that, and by the late 1930s, racing up the steep mountain passes of the Alps, Pyrenees, and Dolomites would never be the same.

Oscar Egg

One common misconception is that Tullio Campagnolo invented the rear derailleur. Although he did invent the quick-release lever in 1930, the derailleur had already been in use by cyclo-tourists since 1905, long before Campagnolo entered the scene. The first derailleur widely used by racers was the one introduced in 1928 by bike shop owner Lucien Joy, and by the mid-'30s his Le Simplex derailleur was found on many racing bikes. In 1937 the Tour de France organizers finally lifted the ban against derailleurs, and Oscar Egg's Super Champion model (a.k.a. Osgear) was used by the victor on every stage of that year's race.

Roger Lapébie claimed victory in the 1937 Tour, and not surprisingly, he set the new average speed record (19.06 mph, 30.67 kmh); besting the previous record (18.66 mph, 30.03 kmh) set the year before. The effect of the derailleur was even more pronounced in the Giro d'Italia, in use there since 1933 - average speeds in Italy's Grand Tour increased by almost 2 mph (3.2 kmh) from 1933 to 1938.

Super Champion rear derailleur

A combination of events would mark the end of the Heroic Era: Gino Bartali's victory in the 1938 Tour de France, thus becoming the first man to win both the Giro and the Tour; the passing of the Tour's founding father, Henri Desgrange, in 1940; and the adoption

Roger Lapebie

of the rear derailleur, punctuated by Roger Lapébie's Tour victory in 1937. Although there is no definitive line in the sand separating the two eras, I have chosen 1935 (the year Bartali earned his first points) as the start for the Modern Era.

In Part 1 I attempted to demonstrate why I chose to create a ranking system for only those riders who belong to the Modern Era of cycling. In the final analysis there proved to be too many differences between the two major time periods. It simply doesn't make much sense to compare someone from the

Heroic Era, such as 1927 and 1928 back-to-back Tour winner Nicolas Frantz, to one of his counterparts from the Modern Era, like Louison Bobet, the first three-time consecutive Tour winner (1953–1955).

To recap, the Heroic Era (pre-1935) was so different from the Modern Era (1935–present) because:

1. Riders rarely traveled to compete in races outside of their home countries.

2. Many important races didn't exist for much of the Heroic Era (including La Flèche-Wallonne, Ghent-Wevelgem, the Vuelta, the classification competitions of the Grand Tours, and most importantly, the World Championships).

3. Many of the great champions perished in World War I.

4. Results in the early part of the era were in large part determined by individual efforts, rather than those of the team.

5. The Tour de France barely resembled the race it later became.

6. Grand Tour champions won either the Tour or Giro, not both.

7. The rear derailleur, along with its huge technological advantage, had yet to gain widespread acceptance in the professional sport.

Nicolas Franz

One day I may go back and rank the riders from cycling's earlier era, but for all the reasons listed above, I have confined my current scoring/ranking system to only those cyclists from the Modern Era. That said, many of the following Heroic Era champions should probably be included when discussing cycling's all-time greats: Lucien Petit-Breton, Octave Lapize, Phillipe Thys, Costante Girardengo, Ottavio Bottecchia, Learco Guerra, Nicolas Frantz, Andre Leducq, Antonin Magne, Sylvère Maes, and of course, Alfredo Binda.

Part II

THE MISSING YEARS:
WAR AND INJURY

The Missing Years:
War and Injury

INTRODUCTION

IN THE FOLLOWING THREE CHAPTERS I'LL BE EXAMINING the missing
years, those years that a cyclist was unable to compete due to war,
injury, or illness. Other ranking systems have been content to simply
acknowledge these gaps in a rider's career and have gone no further.
Considering the huge impact these missing years had on certain
careers, I felt compelled to actually adjust the raw scores cyclists
achieved through my point system. I'll explain the way these points
were awarded, and the adjustments made, in the section on scoring.
Hopefully, some of the following background material will help
explain why I chose such a different path.

Fausto Coppi Crash

The Missing Years:
War and Injury

WORLD WAR II—GINO AND FAUSTO

WORLD WAR II EFFECTIVELY SHUT DOWN professional road racing. The Tour de France was not held from 1940 to 1946, and there were no editions of the Giro d'Italia from 1941 to 1945. Four of cycling's greatest one-day races (Milan-San Remo, Paris-Roubaix, Liège-Bastogne-Liège, and the Giro di Lombardia) all experienced interruptions lasting two to three years. Even when some of the marquee events were still held, there was never a true gathering of the world's best. Fortunately, the greatest champions of the period did survive the war, and even managed to do so with their limbs intact, unlike so many of their counterparts from World War I.

Illustration of Fausto Coppi

Most professionals who had been active at the start of the war had at least five years of their careers carved away, including both Gino Bartali and Fausto Coppi. Certainly, Coppi's *palmarès* would have been far greater, but it was his greatest rival, Bartali, who was actually robbed of his prime cycling years. Gino Bartali turned professional in 1935 and won the Giro d'Italia in 1936 and 1937. He looked well on his way to victory in his first Tour de France appearance in 1937, but when he crashed while descending the Galibier, his injuries eventually forced him to withdraw from the race while still in the yellow jersey. The following year he confirmed his place history by winning the 1938 Tour, becoming the first man to win both of cycling's premier stage races. Gino looked ready to start racking up victories in Grand Tours like no one in the sport before, but in a cruel twist of fate, he would have to wait eight long years to taste victory in another. In 1939 he was prevented from defending his Tour win; the fascist Italian government opted to forego sending their riders to France. A crash in the 1940 Giro effectively took Gino out of contention (young neo-pro Coppi, who Gino himself had recruited, was the eventual winner), and once again Italy would be absent from that year's Tour de France.

By 1941 war had engulfed the entire continent, and Gino Bartali's peak years would forever be lost.

Gino Bartali (Left)

How many more prestigious races might Bartali have won had war not interrupted his career? Certainly, he would have added more Grand Tours, Classics, and perhaps even that missing World Championship title to his long list of victories. Coppi would have had his share of wins, no doubt, but he had just turned pro at the beginning of the war and could well have taken a few years to fully develop. He didn't participate in his first Tour de France until he was twenty-seven (in 1949, which he won).

Lastly, Coppi was very prone to illness and injury; his fragile constitution was perhaps his greatest weakness. Had he raced throughout the war years, there's probably a good chance he would have been sidelined for at least some of the time, for one reason or another. It certainly begs the question: If not for World War II, would it now be Gino Bartali, rather than Fausto Coppi, who is remembered as Italy's greatest cycling legend?

Despite the long five-year break from stage racing, Bartali wasted little time in reminding the cycling world that one of its great champions had returned. In 1946 Gino claimed victory in his first Grand Tour appearance since 1940, defeating none other than his former protégé, Fausto Coppi, at the Giro (by a slim forty-seven-second margin). In 1948 Bartali would again etch his name in the record books when he became the only

Illustration of Gino Bartali

man to go a full decade between Tour de France victories, a record that stands to this day. By that time Gino was in his mid-thirties, and it would be his last Grand Tour victory; his best years were behind him, and Fausto Coppi's had just begun.

The Missing Years: War and Injury

ADDING CONTEXT

ALTHOUGH GINO BARTALI AND FAUSTO COPPI WERE the two most prominent examples of those who had careers interrupted by World War II, two other great cyclists from their era also suffered similar fates—Switzerland's Ferdinand "Ferdi" Kübler and the third great Italian, Fiorenzo Magni. Kübler, who was the Tour winner in 1950 and World Champion of 1951, turned professional in 1940. Magni, who turned pro in 1941, was a three-time Giro champion (1948, 1951, and 1955) and is still the only three-time consecutive Tour of Flanders winner (1949–1951).

Those four great champions all lost roughly five years from their careers, yet still managed to amass an incredible number of victories in the most prestigious races. By the late 1940s they not only had to compete amongst themselves for wins, but by then both Switzerland's Hugo Koblet (the first after Bartali and Coppi to win both the Giro and Tour) and France's Louison Bobet (the first three-time consecutive Tour de France winner, 1953–1955) had also entered the scene; it was truly the Golden Age of Cycling. Once again, we have to wonder just how many more significant wins could have been gained by Bartali, Coppi, Magni, and Kübler from 1941 to 1945 when there were two fewer legends of the sport vying for those same victories.

Illustration of Bartali, Coppi, Magni

Bernard Hinault

To help add some context to all those lost war years, imagine if we were to erase five years of results from two of cycling's more recent legends, Bernard Hinault and Miguel Induráin. Further, how would the *palmarés* of both "The Badger" and "Big Mig" now look if we removed those years when they were at the height of their powers, about six years after they had turned professional, like Bartali's situation? Hinault, who turned pro in 1975, would lose the years from 1981 to 1985. For Induráin, who turned pro in 1984, we would erase the years 1990–1994.

Bernard Hinault won an incredible ten Grand Tours during his career, second only to Eddy Merckx, who claimed eleven victories. He also had nine Classics victories, which included three of the five Monuments (Paris-Roubaix, Liège, and Lombardia). Hinault was also World Champion in 1980. If we were to remove the results of 1981–1985, his list of major accomplishments would have been as follows:

- Tour de France, 1978 and 1979
- Giro d'Italia, 1980
- Vuelta, 1978
- Liège, 1977
- Lombardia, 1979
- World Championship, 1980

Eight of Hinault's twelve Grand Tour podiums would have been erased, along with six of his ten outright victories (three Tours, two Giro, and one Vuelta). Gone too would be his sole Paris-Roubaix victory of 1981. All told, still a very illustrious career, but based on this scoring system, "The Badger" would drop from one of the highest-ranked riders down to around fifteenth place.

Miguel Induráin is the only official five-time consecutive Tour de France winner (1991–1995). During this phenomenal string of victories, he also won the Giro twice, and in back-to-back years for good measure (1992 and 1993). If we were to remove five of his peak years (1990–1994), the results would obviously be devastating. In the end, Induráin would have wound up with only one Tour victory

Miguel Induráin

in 1995 and would not have amassed even enough points to make the list of the Top 100 greatest cyclists. If "Big Mig" had suffered a five-year career interruption in his sixth year as a pro, like Bartali, his true potential would have never been revealed. Induráin's results prior to 1991 were certainly no indication of the dominance that was to follow, as his highest Tour placing up to that point was tenth in 1990.

I am in no way trying to diminish the accomplishments of either Hinault or Induráin in the above examples, but rather illustrating what was potentially lost by all the great champions during the war years. I don't see how any type of ranking system based on points scored in races can properly address this issue unless some type of adjustment is made to compensate for these missing years. I'll lay out my solution to this problem in the next section.

The Missing Years: War and Injury

INJURY

As reviewed in the last two sections, World War II robbed four of the greatest cyclists of the postwar era (Gino Bartali, Fausto Coppi, Ferdi Kübler, and Fiorenzo Magni) of a good portion of their careers. Since I'm going to factor in these missing years when ranking these cyclists against others from the Modern Era, then some consideration should also be given to the other marquee riders who had to contend with injuries, which may have affected their most productive years.

In a horrendous motor-paced track accident in 1969, Eddy Merckx suffered a concussion and a cracked vertebra; worse, his pacer driving the derny was killed instantly. Although it's hard to believe given "The Cannibal's" absolute domination of the sport in the six years following the accident, Merckx claimed he was never the same and suffered for years with back pain, especially while climbing. It's intriguing to think that the most prolific winner of all time could have possibly won even more, or perhaps could have extended his career.

Louison Bobet was tormented by severe saddle sores throughout his career, a condition that ultimately required surgery after he suffered through his win in the 1955 Tour de France. These were no ordinary sores; surgery after the race required 150 stitches to close the gaping

Eddy Merckx

Louison Bobet

wound. Yet, despite this ongoing affliction, Bobet still managed to win three consecutive Tours, a World Championship, and every Monument save Liège. Did his recurring problem cause him to lose out on more victories?

Bernard Hinault and Laurent Fignon were both sidelined by knee injuries. Hinault's injury caused him to abandon the 1980 Tour, although he did go on to win the World Championship later that year. "The Badger" went on to win the Tour in both 1981 and 1982, but the injury flared up again, and he was forced to miss the event in 1983. Hinault returned for the 1984 Tour, but was soundly defeated by the young Fignon, who had also won the previous year in his first attempt at *La Grande Boucle* in Bernard's absence. The tables turned in 1985, and it was Fignon who would sit on the sidelines

Laurent Fignon

with an Achilles injury. Unable to defend his crown, "The Professor" would bear witness to Hinault capturing his fifth, and final, Tour de France. It's fair to say that Fignon never really regained the form from his early career, even though he did go on to claim the 1989 Giro.

None of the great champions mentioned above suffered what could be considered a career-ending injury. The case can certainly be made that Merckx, Bobet, Hinault, and Fignon all could have won more had it not been for their setbacks, but none of them had large chunks of their cycling careers "lost," as did Bartali, Coppi, Kübler, and Magni during World War II. It should also be noted that Coppi struggled throughout his career

Greg LeMond

with both illness and injury, and it's amazing that he was able to accomplish so much given all his bad luck.

This section would not be complete without mentioning the down time of the first non-European cyclist to claim victory in the Tour de France, Greg LeMond. In 1987 he was accidentally shot in a turkey-hunting accident in California while recovering from an injury sustained in the Tirreno-Adriatico race. Subsequent follow-up surgeries, one for gunshot wound complications and the other for knee tendonitis, effectively sidelined him for two years before he returned to the top level of the sport by winning the 1989 Tour de France.

In the end, I have chosen to use a Missing Years adjustment formula to compensate all the following for their career interruptions: Gino Bartali, Fausto Coppi, Ferdinand Kübler, Fiorenzo Magni, Rik Van Steenbergen, Alberic Schotte, Stan Ockers, Marcel Kint, and Greg LeMond. Certainly, this approach is not without its faults, but I think it paints a more accurate picture of the true victory potential of some of cycling's greatest riders.

In the next couple of sections I will outline the entire point scoring system, including the Adjustment Formula mentioned above for "missed years" and all the races I've chosen to include. Hopefully, the last seven sections have lent a bit more clarity to the scoring methodology which will be detailed in Part 3.

Part III

THE SCORING SYSTEM

The Scoring System

SCORING: THE RACES

The scores assigned to the cyclists in this ranking system involve two major components, the first of which I'll cover in this section: the actual races included and the points applied to these events. In the next section I'll cover the special adjustments to the basic scores, which will include Career Milestone Achievements and the Missing Years Adjustment Formula (which I mentioned in the previous section).

I think you'll find that the point values are close to those assigned under the old FICP/UCI ranking system, which is now known as Cycling Quotient, its unofficial successor. The major difference is that I have only awarded points for outright victories (with two major exceptions: all the Grand Tours and the World Championship Road Race). Overall, I think this approach not only emphasizes all the important career highlights of the legends of the sport, but also serves as a simple and straightforward method by which to rank riders. It also helps address the major questions at hand: Who were the best of the best, and who came out victorious more frequently in the races that mattered most?

My goal was to create a somewhat balanced approach that recognized major accomplishments across a broad range of categories: single-day races, time trial events, stage races, the Grand Tours, season-long competitions, and the UCI Hour Record. Most other ranking systems I've encountered place too much emphasis on either the Grand Tours or, conversely, on results in the single-day races. The general idea here was to create a greater awareness of, and appreciation for, those cyclists who have left their mark in a variety of different road events.

Of course, one of the major difficulties encountered when trying to compare careers from different time periods is that races have had varying degrees of importance on the cycling calendar through the years. Some races are now defunct, while others have only recently gained importance or prestige. I've tried to mitigate this situation by including not only a broad range of both single-day races and stage races from all the historically significant cycling regions, but by also choosing events held for approximately forty years (next to each race is its inception date). In the end, I was satisfied that the scoring was balanced across all Modern Era time periods (i.e., the addition of the more recent Clásica de San Sebastián offsets the inclusion Bordeaux–Paris, which is now defunct).

Perhaps the most contentious part of this system is that I have chosen to award bonus points for various Career Milestone Achievements, race records, and the Missing Years Adjustment Formula (applied to compensate those cyclists who lost at least two years of their careers due to war or injury). For the purists, I will include the raw scores achieved by cyclists without any of the special adjustments. but the official rankings will always reflect all components of the scoring system.

Below are all the included races and their assigned points. Again, inception and usual run dates are in parentheses. Also, many of these races have had name changes through the years and are also sometimes known by different names in different countries. I've done my best to include the most currently used names for these races as of year-end 2019. Finally, if you want to see the list of victors for a particular race, I highly recommend BikeRaceInfo.com.

1. The Monuments
Various points

These are the monsters of the single-day races. They have held tremendous importance, and prestige for their victors, throughout the Modern Era and before. With only a handful of exceptions, the great champions usually found a way to win at least one of these storied events. I've opted to give a higher value to Paris-Roubaix, after all, it is the Queen of the Classics. There was a time when the best in the peloton viewed their careers incomplete without a victory in this race. Bernard Hinault despised the cobbles and mud yet knew his place in the hierarchy of legends would have been diminished had he not been first across the Roubaix velodrome finish line at least once in his career—a feat he accomplished in 1981. The case can certainly be made that Paris-Roubaix may not be the most difficult of the Monuments (I believe that honor would go to Flanders, the only one of this group without a four-time winner), but it is without a doubt the most prestigious of the Classics.

- Milan San-Remo (1907, late March), *3 points*
- Tour of Flanders/Ronde van Vlaanderen (1913, early April), *3 points*
- Paris-Roubaix (1896, early April), *4 points*
- Liège-Bastogne-Liège (1892, late April), *3 points*
- Il Lombardia/Giro di Lombardia (1905, early October), *3 points*

2. World Championship Road Race (1927)
4 points (first)
2 points (second)
1 point (third)

Not only have I opted to give the WCRR four points, but I have also chosen to recognize podium places. The extensive list of legendary gold medalists is certainly evidence of the importance of this event. The fact that the race takes place on a different course each year, and is contested by national rather than trade teams, certainly lends to its distinct character. These are also differences that make this a difficult race to capture. Like Flanders, no one has won the event more than three times, but more significantly, only a handful of cyclists have ever made the podium four times, with Alejandro Valverde owning the record at seven appearances. Peter Sagan is the only cyclist to have won three times in a row. Further, two of the greatest Monument champions of all time, Sean Kelly and Roger De Vlaeminck, were winless in the event, a testament to the special difficulties encountered when seeking success in this unique once-a-year battle of the national teams, usually held late in the season in September or October.

3. Classics/Olympics/TT Championships
2 points

One can argue that the Olympic RR is just as difficult to win as the WCRR, but the race has only been open to professionals since 1996, so I'm including it with the other two-point races. Paris-Brussels was once a very prestigious Spring Classic, but after 1966 it lost its shine, due to traffic issues and the growing prestige of the Amstel Gold Race, and was moved from spring to late summer, so only the earlier editions warrant inclusion as a Classic. In its heyday, Zuri-Metzgete was so prestigious, that it was considered the sixth Monument, but now that it's gone the *Clásica de San Sebastián* has grown in prestige and is now considered a summer Classic.

- Olympic Road Race Gold (1996, editions held once every four years)
- Olympic TT Gold (1996, editions held every four years)
- World TT Championships (1994, usually late September or early October)
- Ghent-Wevelgem (1934, late March)
- Amstel Gold (1966, mid to late April)
- La Flèche Wallonne (1936, late April)
- Clásica de San Sebastián (1981, early August)
- Paris-Tours (1896, mid-October)
- Championship of Zurich/Zuri-Metzgete (1917–2006, early October, now an amateur event)
- Paris-Brussels/Brussels Cycling Classic (1893, but only pre-1967 events included in the Classics category, which was held late April)
- Bordeaux–Paris (defunct, 1891–1988, late May)
- Grand Prix de Nations (defunct TT Championship, 1932–2004, September)

4. Semi-Classics/Nationals
1 point

This was a tough category, as I had a difficult time trying to figure out which races to include or exclude. Again, the general rule of

thumb was to include an event that had been in existence for at least forty years; these are the true Semi-Classics, and although they do tend to have somewhat regional biases (i.e., Italians tend to win in Italy and the Belgians in Belgium), they are all prestigious races. There really is a dearth of well-established Spanish one-day races that have been around for a long time, but this is somewhat offset by the higher point totals assigned to Spain's week-long stage races. Also, the Critérium International was known as the Critérium National prior to 1978, and only open to French riders. Once it became an international event, I moved it into the stage race category and assigned it two points. Although relatively unknown now, both the Critérium des As and the Trofeo Angelo Baracchi were prominent year-end events, and since both were by invitation only, just the top cyclists of the season were present; thus, the list of victors is quite illustrious. Lastly, I've included the EuroEyes Cyclassics in this category; it's a young race (1996), but its list of winners is impressive, and it's currently part of
the UCI World Ranking.

- National Championships (various inception dates)
- Omloop Het Nieuwsblad, formerly Het Volk
  (1945, early March)
- Kuurne-Brussels-Kuurne (1946, early March)
- Giro del Lazio/Roma Maxima
  (defunct, 1933–2014, early March)
- Dwars door Vlaanderen (1945, late March)
- Critérium National de la Route
  (defunct, 1932–1978, late March)
- E3 BinckBank Classic, formerly E3 Harelbeke,
  Harelbeke-Antwerp-Harelbeke, E3 Prijs Vlaanderen
  (1958, late March)
- Brabantse Pijl/Flèche Brabanconne (1960, mid-April)
- Scheldeprijs, formerly GP de l'Escaut, Grote Scheldeprijs,
  Scheldeprijs Vlaanderen (1907, mid-April)
- Eschborn-Frankfurt City Loop/Frankfurt GP,
  formerly Rund um den Henninger-Turn (1962, early May)
- Grand Prix of Aargau Canton, formerly GP Gippengen
  (1964, early June)

- EuroEyes Cyclassics, formerly Vattenfall Cyclassics, HEW Cyclassics (1996, late August)
- Bretagne Classic Ouest-France, formerly GP Ouest France, Grand Prix de Plouay (1931, early September)
- Brussels Cycling Classic, formerly Paris-Brussels (1893, post-1966 editions included as a Semi-Classic, early September)
- Grand Prix de Fourmies (1928, early September)
- Giro della Romagna (defunct, 1910–2011, early September)
- Giro della Toscana (1923, mid-September)
- Milano-Torino/Milan-Turin (1876, early October)
- Giro dell'Emilia (1909, early October)
- Tre Valle Varesine (1919, early October)
- Gran Piemonte, formerly Giro del Piemonte (1906, early October)
- Coppa Placci, merged with the Giro del Veneto in 2012 (defunct, 1923–2012, mid-October)
- Giro del Veneto, merged with the Coppa Placci in 2012 (defunct, 1909–2012, mid-October)
- Critérium des As (defunct, 1921–1990, late October)
- Trofeo Angelo Baracchi (defunct, 1946–1990, early November)

5. Minor Tours and Stage Races
2 or 3 points

Three points were given to the more prestigious weeklong stage races, what I call Minor Tours. It may seem odd that the Volta (not to be confused with the Vuelta) was included in this grouping, but its list of winners, and extensive history, convinced me to include it with the other well-known races. It's the third-oldest stage race behind the Tour and the Giro, making its first appearance in 1911.

Three-point races (Minor Tours):

- Paris-Nice (1933, March)
- Tirreno-Adriatico (1966, mid-March)
- Volta a Catalunya/Tour of Catalonia (1911, late March)

- Tour of the Basque Country/Vuelta Ciclista al Pais Vasco (1924, but not held 1931–1934 and 1936–1951, early April)
- Tour of Romandy (1947, late April)
- Tour of Switzerland/Tour de Suisse (1933, June)
- Critérium du Dauphiné,
  formerly Critérium du Dauphiné Libéré (1947, June)

Two-point races:

- Critérium International (defunct, 1978–2016, late March)
- Catalan Week/Setmana Catalunya
  (defunct, 1963–2005, March)
- Settimana Internazionale Coppi e Bartali/Giro di Sardegna (1958, late March)
- Tour of the Alps, formerly Giro del Trentino
  (1979, mid-April)
- Four Days of Dunkirk (1955, early May)
- Tour of Belgium (1908, late May)
- GP Midi Libre (defunct, 1949–2002, June)
- Tour de Luxembourg (1935, early June)
- BinckBank Tour, formerly Eneco Tour of Benelux,
  Ronde van Nederlands (1948, August)

6. Grand Tours
Various points

I'm sure some of you may think the Vuelta has been shortchanged, but it has only been over the last decade that the race has begun to approach the same prestige as the other two Grand Tours. Consider that the Vuelta wasn't even always a three-week stage race and didn't become a fixture on the calendar until 1955. Surely, any number of great riders from the late 1940s and early 1950s, most notably Coppi and Bartali, would have added Spain's Grand Tour to their *palmarés*, had the race been held on a regular basis. Although it has been considered a Grand Tour since the 1950s, the race gradually become more prestigious throughout the 1960s. It wasn't until 1974 that the race was regularly held with twenty stages, thus becoming a true Grand Tour. It is for this reason that I've opted to increase the point totals starting in that year. The case can be made that since ASO (Amaury Sport Organization, owner of the Tour de France) acquired 49 percent of the event in 2008 and full control in 2014, the Vuelta has started to approach the same level of importance on the calendar as the Giro. The UCI currently issues the same number of points to the winners and podium spots of both the Giro and Vuelta, but I have chosen to assign lower point totals for the Spanish Grand Tour; that may change in future ranking calculations.

As with the World Champ RR, points have been awarded for the podium spots in all the Grand Tours due to the importance of these events.

- Giro d'Italia/Tour of Italy (1909, May)
  6 points (first); 3 points (second); 1 point (third)
- Tour de France (1903, July) *8 points (first);
  4 points (second); 2 points (third)*
- Vuelta a España/Tour of Spain (1935, but race not held from 1937 to 1940, 1943–1944, 1949, and 1951–1954, August/September) *Pre-1974 4 points (first);
  2 points (second); 1 point (third)*
  *1974–present 5 points (first); 2 points (second);
  1 point (third)*

7. Grand Tour Classifications
2 points (mountains, points)

I've opted to award two points for both the mountains and points classifications for each of the three Grand Tours. I do realize that each Grand Tour has used varying formulas to assign the points which were totaled in order to declare the winner of these competitions over the years; it is quite possible that a uniform method of calculation for each classification would have produced different winners in certain years. In the end, awarding the same number of points for the two major GT classifications seemed to make the most sense.

- Giro, mountains classification (1933)
- Giro, points classification (1966)
- Tour, mountains classification (1933)
- Tour, points classification (1953)
- Vuelta, mountains classification (1935)
- Vuelta, points classification (1945)

8. GT Stage wins
½ point

These victories include all Grand Tour stages, including prologues, time trials, team time trials, and regular stages. This was another category that was a bit tricky to settle on a proper point value. I was originally going to go with one point for each stage win, but doing so really altered the final standings; it created an imbalance in the overall scoring, placing too much of an emphasis on results in Grand Tours. It is also worth noting that there is a completely different dynamic involved when going for victory in a stage of a Grand Tour. Oftentimes the fight for the leader's jersey will dictate whether another member of the team is even allowed to challenge for the win in a given stage, especially if there are time bonuses involved. There were certainly situations when the strongest rider on any given day was not able to vie for victory, due to tactics related to the general classification battle. Also, I realize not all Grand Tour stages were created equal, and without doubt, certain stages carry far greater prestige for the victor, usually famed mountaintop finishes. Once again, I opted for simplicity here and just awarded the same points across the board. I do think it all balances out in the end; the great sprinters rack up their points and get a bonus for winning points classifications, and the famed mountain men usually get a high place on GC or capture the mountains classification.

9. Season-Long Competitions
2 points

Although many of the winners of these titles didn't necessarily target these competitions, especially since the UCI took over their management in 1989, the cyclists are most of the same names who appear on the final Top 100 list. Oddly, there were actually two season-long competitions covering a twenty-year span. Both the Super Prestige Pernod Trophy (1959–1987) and the UCI Road World Cup (1988–1904) were run parallel to the UCI World Road Rankings, which also covered the years from 1984 to 2004; the two former competitions covered just certain events, whereas the latter covered all UCI-sanctioned races for the entire calendar year. Currently there are once again two season-long competitions: the UCI World Tour, only covering certain events, and the UCI World Rankings, which cover all UCI-sanctioned races. I know, it's confusing, and I wish the UCI would just award one title to a single rider at the end of the season.

- Unofficial Season-Long Competition (1936–1939, 1946, and 1947)
- Desgrange-Colombo Trophy (1948–1958)
- Super Prestige Pernod Trophy (1959–1987)
- UCI Road World Cup (1988–2004)
- UCI World Road Rankings (1984–2004)
- UCI ProTour Competition (2005–2008)
- UCI World Tour (2009–present)
- UCI World Ranking (2016–present)

10. Hour Record
3 points

Yes, technically this is a track event, but a roadie has almost always held the record, so I've opted to include it. Since 1972 I've only included the UCI record (riders are restricted to using roughly the same equipment that Merckx used in his record-breaking 1972 attempt) and the newer UCI unified record (in line with regulations for current track pursuit bikes).

- Hour Record (prior to 1972)
- UCI Record/"Merckx Record" (1972–2014)
- UCI Unified Record (2014–present)

That is the basic framework for earning the raw scores issued in *Peloton Legends*. The next section will review the bonus points earned for Significant Lifetime Achievements and the Missing Years Adjustment Formula.

The Scoring System

SCORING: THE ADJUSTMENTS

THIS SECTION WILL COMPLETE THE SCORING SYSTEM that has been
developed to rank the Top 100 cyclists. In the previous section the
races that form the cyclist's raw scores were outlined.

As a refresher, points were earned by victories in the following ten
categories:

- The Monuments
- The World Championship Road Race*
- Classics/Olympics/TT Championships
- Semi-Classics/National Championships
- Minor Tours and Stage Races
- Grand Tours*
- Grand Tour Classifications (Mountains and Points)
- Grand Tour Stages
- Season Long Competitions
- Bonus: The UCI World Hour Record

Career Milestone Achievements and Adjustments

After I had completed the basic scoring sheets for all the top cyclists
of the Modern Era, it was a lot easier to compare all the greats;
I now had a nice snapshot of an entire career, as all their major
victories had been grouped into these various categories (along
with the points earned in each). Every other historical source I'd
consulted provided career wins (*palmarès*) in a year-by-year format.
When I began evaluating victories grouped by type of race, this
new perspective started to reveal some rather significant career
achievements, which had been somewhat hidden by the standard
yearly results format. Some of these milestones are quite well known
and often discussed, while others may come as a complete surprise
to even the most diehard of fans.

It was these hidden major accomplishments that convinced me there
was far more to a cyclist's career than the sum of their victories.
This may be stating the obvious when it comes to the well-known
greats, but I was surprised by some of the significant achievements
of some of the less well-known champions of the Modern Era, such
as Jan Janssen. In the final analysis, I felt that these special lifetime
accomplishments warranted extra points in addition to the raw

---

[1] *Points also awarded for podium spots.*

scores achieved through victories in the most significant races. I know not everyone is going to agree with this approach, but I believe this method provides a more accurate representation of a cyclist's true standing in the pecking order of all-time greats.

I created three separate categories of special career achievements and adjustments. One for single-day races, another for Grand Tours, and finally a combined category. Further, each category includes three different milestone accomplishments. My goal was to make sure that I didn't tip the scale in favor of single-day specialists or Grand Tour specialists. The rule of thumb was that if there were more than ten cyclists who had achieved an accomplishment up for consideration, I decided it was no longer unique, thus no longer "special," and it was eliminated from inclusion. Conversely, I didn't want to choose milestones that were so exclusive that only one cyclist made the cut; there were any number of special achievements that could have been created just for Eddy Merckx.

The points awarded for each bonus were based on the number of cyclists who qualified for each adjustment. If there were four or fewer cyclists, fifteen points were awarded; five to six cyclists, twelve points; and seven to ten cyclists, ten points. I spent months poring over statistics and race results before finally choosing the final nine special achievements; this part of the scoring system was without a doubt the most difficult piece of this entire project.

I've also opted to award extra points for the record holders of the twelve most significant races; after all, these are special career achievements, as well. These include all five Monuments, the World Championship Road Race, and all three Grand Tours. The extra points given were the same as those awarded for a single victory in each respective race (see the previous chapter). In the event there were multiple record holders for a race, each was given the same number of points.

Finally, I've decided to create a Missing Years Adjustment Formula, which is my way of compensating those cyclists who lost at least two years of their careers due to war or injury. The math behind the additional points that were awarded is at the end of this chapter.

Career Milestone Adjustments

Single-Day Races

- Won all five Monuments, *15 points*:
  Rik Van Looy, Eddy Merckx, Roger De Vlaeminck

- Twenty-five combined wins in all major single-day
  race categories (Monuments, World Championship
  Road Race, Classics, and Semi-Classics), *10 points*:
  Gino Bartali, Fausto Coppi, Van Looy, Merckx,
  De Vlaeminck, Francesco Moser, Johan Museeuw,
  Tom Boonen

- Won thirty Grand Tour stages, 10 points:
  Delio Rodriguez, Coppi, Van Looy, Merckx,
  Freddy Maertens, Bernard Hinault, Mario Cipollini,
  Alessandro Petacchi, Mark Cavendish

Grand Tours (Giro d'Italia, Tour de France, Vuelta a España)

- Won eight GTs, *15 points*:
  Jacques Anquetil, Merckx, Hinault

- Won all three GTs, *10 points*:
  Anquetil, Felice Gimondi, Merckx, Hinault,
  Alberto Contador, Vincenzo Nibali, Chris Froome

- Won eight GT Classifications (Points or Mountain,
  any combination), *10 points*:
  Bartali, Federico Bahamontes, Merckx, Lucien Van Impe,
  Sean Kelly, Laurent Jalabert, Erik Zabel

Combined Category (Single-Day Races + Grand Tours)

- Achieved at least one victory in every major road category (Monuments, WCRR, Classics, Semi-Classics, Minor Tours, Grand Tours, GT Classification Competitions, GT Stages, and Season-Long Competitions), *10 points*: Louison Bobet, Ferdi Kübler, Jan Janssen, Merckx, Hinault, Moser, Alejandro Valverde
- Won three of any five different Monuments and any GT, *10 points*: Coppi, Bobet, Merckx, Gimondi, Hinault, Moser, Kelly
- 150 or more career road victories, *10 points*: Van Looy, Merckx, De Vlaeminck, Kelly, Moser, Cipollini, André Greipel

Jan Janssen

Race Records

- Milan San-Remo (*3 points*): Seven wins—Merckx
- Ronde van Vlaanderen/Tour of Flanders (*3 points*): Three wins—Achiel Buysse, Fiorenzo Magni, Eric Leman, Johan Museeuw, Boonen, Fabian Cancellara
- Paris-Roubaix (*4 points*): Four wins—De Vlaeminck and Boonen
- Liège-Bastogne-Liège (*3 points*): Five wins—Merckx

Felice Gimondi

- World Road Race Championship (4 *points*):
  Three wins—Alfredo Binda*, Rik Van Steenbergen,
  Merckx, Óscar Freire, Peter Sagan
- Giro di Lombardia/Tour of Lombardy (3 *points*):
  Five wins—Coppi
- Giro d'Italia/Tour of Italy (6 *points*):
  Five wins—Alfredo Binda*, Coppi, and Merckx
- Tour de France (8 *points*):
  Five wins—Anquetil, Merckx, Hinault, and Miguel Induráin
- Vuelta a Espagña/Tour of Spain (4 *points*):
  Four wins—Roberto Heras

Missing Years Adjustment

- Gino Bartali, 48.5 points
- Fausto Coppi, 36 points
- Ferdi Kübler, 16 points
- Fiorenzo Magni, 21 points
- Alberic Schotte, 9 points
- Marcel Kint, 9.5 points
- Stan Ockers, 6 points
- Rik Van Steenbergen, 7 points
- Greg LeMond, 13 points

---

*Binda is part of the Heroic Era (pre-1935) and is not part of this scoring system

Missing Years Formula

Do not continue reading this section unless you are an analytic, number-crunching geek. So, for those who would like to know how I arrived at the above added points, read on. First off, my objective with this adjustment was to answer a huge "what if . . . ." What if all the above cyclists had been healthy and racing during their years lost to war, injury, or illness? Just how many additional points might they have scored, extrapolated from their points earned during their productive years? Productive years—that is the key to this equation. Many cyclists hung on well past their ability to win races. The best example is Rik Van Steenbergen. He turned pro in 1943 and won his last race (of those available in this scoring system) in 1958, yet he did not retire until 1966. In other words, for eight of Steenbergen's twenty-four years as a pro, he didn't win a single race included in this scoring system. I don't think it would make a lot of sense to include those final eight years if we are trying to determine what he might have won during his productive "missing years" lost to World War II from 1943 to 1945. So, when I'm calculating average points scored during a career, "career" is defined as follows: the year a cyclist turned professional through the last year points were earned in a qualifying race. So here is the formula:

1. Length of career (defined above)

2. Subtract from step 1 the number of "missing years"

3. Average number of points scored in a cyclist's scoring career (rider's raw score divided by the total from step 2)

4. Number from step 3 multiplied by the number of missing years (this will equal the number of points a cyclist could have scored during his missing years)

5. Subtract from step 4 any points scored during the missing years (i.e., Van Steenbergen won the Belgian Nationals in 1943 and Flanders in 1944, one of the rare big-time races that took place during the war years).

6.   If the missing years took place during the cyclist's first five years as a professional, then they received 75 percent of the figure from step 5. If the missed years took place during a cyclist's prime, five years after turning professional, then they received 100 percent of the total from step 5.

7.   Finally, the number from step 6 is rounded to the nearest whole number.

Yes, I know this is a bit like filling out an income tax return, but here is an example using Rik Van Steenbergen (who was professional from 1943 to 1966):

1.   Scoring career: 1943–1958, 16 years (last point scored was in '58 Critérium de As) Missing years: 3 years (1943–1945)

2.   Actual number of scoring years: 13 (16 − 3)
Raw score of *62.5 points* (all points earned over entire scoring career)

3.   Average number of points scored during scoring career: *4.8 (62.5 / 13)*

4.   Hypothetical points scored during missing years: *14.4 (4.80 x 3)* Actual points scored during missing years: *5* (Belgium National Champ in 1943, 1945; Flanders in 1944)

5.   Adjustment for points scored during missing years: *9.4 points (14.4 - 5)*

6.   Adjustment, as missed years were during cyclist's first five years: *7.05 points (.75 x 9.4)*

7.   Rounded to nearest whole number: *7 points*

There, see how easy that was?

Rik Van Steenbergen (Right)

Part IV

THE TOP 100 CYCLISTS
OF THE MODERN ERA

The Top 100 Cyclists of the Modern Era

PELOTON LEGENDS OFFICIAL RANKINGS

ON THE FOLLOWING THREE PAGES ARE THE FINAL RANKINGS of the
Top 100 Cyclists of the Modern Era, as of year-end 2019. The final
point totals include all those earned in a cyclist's professional career
as outlined in the previous two chapters. Keep in mind these totals
include not only the points earned from race results, but also the
Career Milestone Adjustments, Race Records, and the Missing Years
Adjustment. If you'd like to know which cyclists received any of
these extra points and why they were awarded, please refer to the
previous section.

The list was first sorted by Total Score. If there was a tie in points,
then the cyclist with the greater raw score was ranked higher. If
there was still a tie in points after that filter, then the cyclist with the
greater number of career wins was ranked higher.

The column labeled "wins" includes professional road victories
only. Depending on the source referenced, a cyclist's total victory
count can include just about any type races, which can include all
the following: amateur and kermess, six-day, cyclocross, and post
Tour de France Critériums. You'll find that my totals rarely match
up with what is usually included on Wikipedia, which almost never
sites a source for the total number of victories quoted in the cyclist's
entry. I have chosen to use a single source for all wins in Peloton
Legends—ProCyclingStats.com (PCS). PCS includes every race that
is part of this scoring system, but where I do differ with PCS is that I
have chosen to include team time trial (TTT) wins in all three Grand
Tours as part of the total career victory counts, whereas PCS doesn't.

If a cyclist received a suspension from the sport's governing body,
the UCI, and had race results stripped from the record books, the
rankings will reflect the removal of any points earned from those
victories. The subject of doping is addressed in detail after the
ranking pages.

RANK	CYCLIST	TOTAL POINTS	RAW SCORE	COUNTRY	WINS	YEARS ACTIVE
1	EDDY MERCKX	418.5	294.5	BELGIUM	292	65-78
2	BERNARD HINAULT	232.5	169.5	FRANCE	149	75-86
3	FAUSTO COPPI	220.5	145.5	ITALY	92	39-59
4	GINO BARTALI	213.0	144.5	ITALY	87	35-54
5	JACQUES ANQUETIL	191.5	158.5	FRANCE	132	54-69
6	SEAN KELLY	169.5	139.5	IRELAND	160	77-94
7	FRANCESCO MOSER	156.5	116.5	ITALY	152	73-88
8	ROGER DE VLAEMINCK	153.0	114.0	BELGIUM	164	69-84
9	RIK VAN LOOY	152.0	107.0	BELGIUM	165	53-70
10	ALEJANDRO VALVERDE	115.0	105.0	SPAIN	129	02-PRESENT
11	MIGUEL INDURÁIN	112.0	104.0	SPAIN	91	84-96
12	FELICE GIMONDI	112.0	92.0	ITALY	78	65-79
13	LOUISON BOBET	103.5	83.5	FRANCE	63	47-61
14	LAURENT JALABERT	99.5	89.5	FRANCE	141	89-02
15	FREDDY MAERTENS	99.0	89.0	BELGIUM	148	72-85
16	CHRIS FROOME	98.5	88.5	GREAT BRITAIN	47	07-PRESENT
17	FERDI KÜBLER	94.5	68.5	SWITZERLAND	71	40-57
18	TONY ROMINGER	90.5	90.5	SWITZERLAND	94	86-97
19	FIORENZO MAGNI	87.5	63.5	ITALY	56	41-56
20	GIUSEPPE SARONNI	86.5	86.5	ITALY	145	77-89
21	ALBERTO CONTADOR	84.5	74.5	SPAIN	70	03-17
22	JOOP ZOETEMELK	84.0	84.0	NETHERLANDS	97	70-87
23	VINCENZO NIBALI	82.0	72.0	ITALY	55	05-PRESENT
24	ERIK ZABEL	76.0	66.0	GERMANY	144	92-08
25	TOM BOONEN	76.0	59.0	BELGIUM	121	02-17

RANK	CYCLIST	TOTAL POINTS	RAW SCORE	COUNTRY	WINS	YEARS ACTIVE
26	RIK VAN STEENBERGEN	73.5	62.5	BELGIUM	63	43-66
27	MARIO CIPOLLINI	73.5	53.5	ITALY	167	89-05
28	RAYMOND POULIDOR	70.5	70.5	FRANCE	73	60-77
29	JOHAN MUSEEUW	70.0	57.0	BELGIUM	68	88-04
30	GREG LEMOND	66.0	53.0	USA	33	81-94
31	PETER SAGAN	65.0	61.0	SLOVAKIA	113	09-PRESENT
32	JAN JANSSEN	63.0	53.0	NETHERLANDS	46	62-72
33	LAURENT FIGNON	62.5	62.5	FRANCE	60	82-93
34	LUIS OCAÑA	59.5	59.5	SPAIN	60	68-77
35	PAOLO BETTINI	59.0	59.0	ITALY	61	97-08
36	FABIAN CANCELLARA	59.0	56.0	SWITZERLAND	87	01-16
37	CHARLY GAUL	57.5	57.5	LUXEMBOURG	48	53-65
38	FRANCO BITOSSI	57.0	57.0	ITALY	98	61-78
39	MARK CAVENDISH	56.5	46.5	GREAT BRITAIN	149	05-PRESENT
40	GIANNI BUGNO	54.5	54.5	ITALY	59	85-98
41	PHILIPPE GILBERT	52.5	52.5	BELGIUM	77	02-PRESENT
42	JAN RAAS	51.5	51.5	NETHERLANDS	68	75-85
43	MORENO ARGENTIN	51.0	51.0	ITALY	69	80-94
44	CLAUDIO CHIAPPUCCI	50.5	50.5	ITALY	33	85-98
45	JAN ULLRICH	50.5	50.5	GERMANY	31	94-06
46	FEDERICO BAHAMONTES	50.5	40.5	SPAIN	41	54-65
47	LUCIEN VAN IMPE	50.0	40.0	BELGIUM	30	69-87
48	STEPHEN ROCHE	49.5	49.5	IRELAND	52	81-93
49	ALEX ZULLE	48.0	48.0	SWITZERLAND	65	91-04
50	HUGO KOBLET	48.0	48.0	SWITZERLAND	55	46-58

RANK	CYCLIST	TOTAL POINTS	RAW SCORE	COUNTRY	WINS	YEARS ACTIVE
51	JOAQUIN RODRIGUEZ	48.0	48.0	SPAIN	48	01-16
52	HERMAN VAN SPRINGEL	47.0	47.0	BELGIUM	64	65-81
53	NAIRO QUINTANA	47	47	COLOMBIA	41	09-PRESENT
54	ALESSANDRO PETACCHI	47.0	37.0	ITALY	149	96-15
55	ALBERIC SCHOTTE	46.5	37.5	BELGIUM	25	40-59
56	MICHELE BARTOLI	46.0	46.0	ITALY	53	93-04
57	CADEL EVANS	45.0	45.0	AUSTRALIA	35	99-15
58	ÓSCAR FREIRE	44.5	40.5	SPAIN	71	98-12
59	BERNARD THÉVENET	43.0	43.0	FRANCE	53	70-81
60	WALTER GODEFROOT	42.5	42.5	BELGIUM	61	65-79
61	CHARLY MOTTET	40.0	40.0	FRANCE	58	83-94
62	ALEXANDRE VINOKOUROV	38.0	38.0	KAZAKHSTAN	54	98-12
63	VITTORIO ADORNI	37.5	37.5	ITALY	42	61-70
64	FRANCESCO CASAGRANDE	37.5	37.5	ITALY	41	93-05
65	STAN OCKERS	37.5	31.5	BELGIUM	20	41-56
66	FRED DE BRUYNE	37.0	37.0	BELGIUM	23	53-61
67	ROBERTO HERAS	37.0	32.0	SPAIN	23	95-05
68	PEDRO DELGADO	36.5	36.5	SPAIN	25	82-94
69	JOSE MANUEL FUENTE	35.5	35.5	SPAIN	21	70-76
70	MARCEL KINT	35.5	26.0	BELGIUM	25	35-51
71	DELIO RODRIGUEZ	35.0	25.5	SPAIN	117	39-49
72	RUDI ALTIG	35.0	35.0	GERMANY	66	60-71
73	GIANBATTISTA BARONCHELLI	34.5	34.5	ITALY	57	74-89
74	GIANNI MOTTA	34.5	34.5	ITALY	52	64-74
75	DAMINO CUNEGO	34	34	ITALY	47	02-18

RANK	CYCLIST	TOTAL POINTS	RAW SCORE	COUNTRY	WINS	YEARS ACTIVE
76	BRADLEY WIGGINS	34.0	34.0	GREAT BRITAIN	33	01-16
77	JULIAN BERRENDERO	33.0	33.0	SPAIN	51	35-49
78	MARCO PANTANI	32.5	32.5	ITALY	30	93-03
79	GERRIE KNETEMANN	31.5	31.5	NETHERLANDS	73	74-89
80	GILBERTO SIMONI	31.5	31.5	ITALY	24	94-10
81	HENNIE KUIPER	31.5	31.5	NETHERLANDS	19	73-88
82	DAVIDE REBELLIN	30.5	30.5	ITALY	60	92-PRESENT
83	DANILO DI LUCA	30.5	30.5	ITALY	43	98-13
84	GREG VAN AVERMAET	30.5	30.5	BELGIUM	43	06-PRESENT
85	ABRAHAM OLANO	30.0	30.0	SPAIN	48	92-02
86	PASCAL RICHARD	30.0	30.0	SWITZERLAND	43	86-00
87	ANDRE DARRIGADÉ (TIE)	29.5	29.5	FRANCE	60	51-66
87	MIGUEL POBLET (TIE)	29.5	29.5	SPAIN	60	52-62
89	ERCOLE BALDINI	29.5	29.5	ITALY	31	57-64
90	ROBBIE MCEWEN	29.0	29.0	AUSTRALIA	115	96-12
91	ROLF SØRENSEN	29.0	29.0	DENMARK	54	86-02
92	NINO DEFILIPPIS	29.0	29.0	ITALY	42	52-64
93	GASTONE NENCINI	28.5	28.5	ITALY	16	53-65
94	RICHARD VIRENQUE	28	28	FRANCE	22	91-04
95	ANDRÉ GREIPEL	28.0	18.0	GERMANY	156	02-PRESENT
96	MAURIZIO FONDRIEST	27.5	27.5	ITALY	56	87-98
97	IVAN BASSO	27.5	27.5	ITALY	33	99-15
98	MICHAEL POLLENTIER	27	27	BELGIUM	42	73-84
99	PRIMOŽ ROGLIČ	27.0	27.0	SLOVENIA	35	13-PRESENT
100	MARINO LEJARRETA	26.5	26.5	FRANCE	55	79-92

The Top 100 Cyclists of the Modern Era

DOPING

As previously mentioned, these rankings include only official race results, and as such, are affected by the removal of rather significant victories as part of the terms of a sanction issued by the sport's governing body, the UCI, for doping violations.

Doping has existed in the sport from the beginning, is currently in use, and will unfortunately probably always be part of professional cycling. That is stating the obvious, but I feel strongly that some distinction must be made when discussing the various types drug use, particularly the oxygen vector doping (OVD) introduced in early 1990s that became such a game changer. The two most prominent forms of OVD, erythropoietin (EPO) and blood transfusions, provided benefits to endurance athletes that simply didn't exist with earlier forms of banned substances like amphetamines, painkillers, testosterone, or steroids. Unlike all the previous drugs taken by cyclists, studies of EPO have demonstrated gains of up to 12 percent to an athlete's aerobic capacity. Even if the boost from using this drug was limited to just 5 percent, it is my belief that EPO, and to a lesser extent blood doping, actually created Grand Tour champions, certain cyclists who would have never otherwise won these races without these forms of performance enhancements.

Without getting into a detailed history of oxygen vector doping, Dr. Francesco Conconi and his assistants (most notably Luigi Cecchini and Michele Ferrari) at the University of Ferrara in Northern Italy helped introduce EPO to the peloton in the early 1990s, and by the middle of the decade, it's safe to say the clear majority were on the drug. I agree with Patrick Brady from the website Red Kite Prayer— Gianni Bugno, an early client of Dr. Conconi, was more than likely the first cyclist to win a Grand Tour with the assistance of EPO in the 1990 Giro d'Italia.

First, consider Bugno's Giro track record prior to that victory: forty-first in his first attempt in 1986, a withdrawal in both '87 and '88, and then twenty-third place in '89. Bugno then went on to wear the leader's pink jersey in the 1990 Giro from beginning to end, a demonstration of dominance last accomplished by none other than Eddy Merckx in 1973. This oddity of coming from practical

Forced from the sport too early, Charly Mottet

anonymity to become a Grand Tour contender was repeated by two more of Conconi's well-known clients, Claudio Chiapucci, and significantly, Miguel Induráin.

The often-repeated saw "everyone is doping, so everyone is on a level playing field" was far from the truth at the advent of the EPO boom. In the early 1990s there were clearly those who were not taking part in oxygen vector doping. It wasn't a level playing field at all. The transition to OVD had to have put a dent in the career victory tally of those talented riders who chose not to participate in doping or simply didn't have access to EPO. I believe all the following were unfairly handicapped during the early adoption of phases of OVD and were prematurely forced out of the sport: Charly Mottet, who was the first runner-up to Bugno in his 1990 Giro rampage; Luis Herrera, the only cyclist after Federico Bahamontes to win the mountains classification in all three Grand Tours; Andy Hampsten,

Another casualty of the doping era, Luis Herrera.

winner of the 1988 Giro; Edwig Van Hooydonk, winner of the 1989 and 1991 Tour of Flanders; and lastly, Greg LeMond, a three-time Tour de France winner. All five of those cyclists effectively had their careers cut short or had their places in this ranking system affected by the dawn of the EPO era. There is enough anecdotal evidence to support the conclusion that each of them was not taking part in the new forms of doping, and they would have undoubtedly racked up far greater points had they jumped on the EPO bandwagon.

Of course, no doping discussion would be complete without including Lance Armstrong. I mentioned him a couple of times in the introduction, but almost nowhere else does his name appear. Some might find it odd that Miguel Induráin is featured prominently, even though I just alluded to the fact that all his Tour victories might have been "assisted" as well. The fact of the matter is that Armstrong had his Tour victories stripped by the UCI and

"Big Mig" did not. Despite all of his annulled results after 1998, Armstrong is still the official winner of the following races in this point scoring system: US Road Race Championship and World RR Championship in 1993, the Clásica de San Sebastián in 1995, Flèche Wallonne in 1996, and the Tour of Luxembourg in 1998. Those wins are not nearly enough to get Armstrong anywhere close to being in the Top 100. For those who are interested in knowing where he would have ranked had none of his results been voided, he would have ended up in tenth place (as of year-end 2019) with 116.5 points. Certainly, a legendary career, but his was never a name that should have been mentioned as the greatest ever; he simply didn't enter and win enough races.

I'm not exactly a big fan of those cyclists who made the Top 100 from the EPO/blood doping era, which I estimate was at its peak from about 1990–2010. This is particularly true of those riders who rose to prominence at the beginning of this era, only to fade when most of the peloton also participated in the same doping regimens. We now know that the drug testing during that early adoption period for such practices was also horribly ineffective or nonexistent. That said, no attempt was made in structuring the points, or picking which races to include, to disadvantage any cyclist from those two decades.

It's a shame to think that a cyclist who may have been the next Fausto Coppi was possibly driven from the sport by a refusal to use something like EPO. If that did indeed happen, we can thank the doctors who introduced oxygen vector doping to the peloton. I'm hopeful that the sport has crossed the threshold into a new era. I don't kid myself by thinking doping is ever going to be eradicated, but just maybe the tests developed to catch it will prevent a repeat of what happened when EPO use was rampant—an entire generation of cycling results that must now be singled out and marked with an ugly asterisk.

Also robbed of victories, Edwig Van Hooydonck (Above) and Andy Hampsten (Below)

Part V

THE TOP 50: CAREER HIGHLIGHTS
AND SCORING SHEETS

The Top 50

CAREER HIGHLIGHTS AND SCORING SHEETS

IN THIS SECTION YOU WILL FIND SUMMARIES of the Top 50 cyclist's careers and their scoring sheets, which will include the points earned in all the races included in this scoring system.

I'll eventually be releasing the career summaries and scoring sheets for the rest of the Top 100 through the *Peloton Legends* website, PelotonLegends.com.

Fiorenzo Magni

MASTER SCORING SHEET

THE MONUMENTS	
RACE	**POINTS**
MILAN–SAN REMO:	3
TOUR OF FLANDERS/RONDE VAN VLAANDEREN	3
PARIS–ROUBAIX	4
LIÈGE-BASTOGNE-LIÈGE	3
IL LOMBARDIA/GIRO DI LOMBARDIA	3

WORLD CHAMPIONSHIP ROAD RACE	
RACE	**POINTS**
GOLD	4
SILVER	2
BRONZE	1

CLASSICS/OLYMPICS/TIME TRIALS	
RACE	**POINTS**
OLYMPIC ROAD RACE GOLD	2
OLYMPIC TT GOLD	2
WORLD TT GOLD	2
GHENT–WEVELGEM	2
AMSTEL GOLD	2
LA FLÈCHE WALLONNE	2
CLÁSICA DE SAN SEBASTIÁN	2
PARIS–TOURS	2
CHAMPIONSHIP OF ZURICH/ZURI-METZGETE	2
PARIS–BRUSSELS (PRE 1966 EDITIONS)	2
BORDEAUX-PARIS	2
GRAND PRIX DE NATIONS	2

SEMI-CLASSICS/NATIONALS	
RACE	POINTS
NATIONAL CHAMPIONSHIPS	I
OMLOOP HET NIEUWSBLAD/HET VOLK	I
KUURNE–BRUSSELS–KUURNE	I
GIRO DEL LAZIO/ROMA MAXIMA	I
DWARS DOOR VLAANDEREN	I
CRITÉRIUM NATIONAL DE LA ROUTE	I
E3 BINKBANK CLASSIC/E3 HARELBEKE/HARELBEKE–ANTWERP–HARELBEKE/E3 PRIJS VLAANDEREN	I
BRABANTSE PIJL/FLÈCHE BRABANÇONNE	I
SCHELDEPRIJS/GP DE L'ESCAUT/GROTE SCHELDEPRIJS/SCHELDEPRIJS VLAANDEREN	I
ESCHBORN-FRANKFURT/FRANKFURT GRAND PRIX/RUND UM DEN HENNINGER-TURN	I
GRAND PRIX OF AARGAU CANTON/GP GIPPENGEN	I
EUROEYES CYCLASSICS/VATTENFALL CYCLASSICS, HEW CYCLASSICS	I
BRETAGNE CLASSIC OUEST–FRANCE/GP OUEST–FRANCE/GRAND PRIX DE PLOUAY	I
BRUSSELS CYCLING CLASSIC/PARIS–BRUSSELS (POST 1966 EDITIONS)	I
GRAND PRIX DE FOURMIES	I
GIRO DELLA ROMAGNA	I
GIRO DELLA TOSCANA	I
MILANO–TORINO/MILAN–TURIN	I
GIRO DELL'EMILIA	I
TRE VALLE VARESINE	I
GRAN PIEMONTE/GIRO DEL PIEMONTE	I

MASTER SCORING SHEET (CONTINUED)

SEMI-CLASSICS/NATIONALS (CONTINUED)	
RACE	POINTS
COPPA PLACCI	I
GIRO DEL VENETO	I
CRITÉRIUM DES AS	I
TROFEO BARACCHI	I

MINOR TOURS AND STAGE RACES	
RACE	POINTS
PARIS-NICE	3
TIRRENO-ADRIATICO	3
VOLTA A CATALUNYA/TOUR OF CATALONIA	3
TOUR OF THE BASQUE COUNTRY/VUELTA CICLISTA AL PAIS VASCO	3
TOUR OF ROMANDY	3
CRITÉRIUM DU DAUPHINÉ/CRITÉRIUM DU DAUPHINÉ LIBÉRÉ	3
TOUR OF SWITZERLAND/TOUR DE SUISSE	3
CRITÉRIUM INTERNATIONAL	2
CATALAN WEEK/SETMANA CATALUNYA	2
SETTIMANA INTERNAZIONALE COPPI E BARTALI/GIRO DI SARDEGNA	2
TOUR OF THE ALPS/GIRO DEL TRENTINO	2
FOUR DAYS OF DUNKIRK	2
TOUR OF BELGIUM	2
GP MIDI LIBRE	2
TOUR DE LUXEMBOURG	2
BINCKBANK TOUR/ENECO TOUR OF BENELUX/RONDE VAN NEDERLANDS	2

GRAND TOURS	
RACE	POINTS
GIRO D'ITALIA - 1ST PLACE	6
GIRO D'ITALIA - 2ND PLACE	3
GIRO D'ITALIA - 3RD PLACE	1
TOUR DE FRANCE - 1ST PLACE	8
TOUR DE FRANCE - 2ND PLACE	4
TOUR DE FRANCE - 3RD PLACE	2
VUELTA A ESPAÑA (TOUR OF SPAIN) - 1ST PLACE (PRE 1974)	4
VUELTA A ESPAÑA (TOUR OF SPAIN) - 1ST PLACE (1974-PRESENT)	5
VUELTA A ESPAÑA (TOUR OF SPAIN) - 2ND PLACE	2
VUELTA A ESPAÑA (TOUR OF SPAIN) - 3RD PLACE	1
GRAND TOUR CLASSIFICATION JERSEYS	
RACE	POINTS
GIRO D'ITALIA: POINTS	2
TOUR DE FRANCE: POINTS	2
VUELTA A ESPAÑA: POINTS	2
GIRO D'ITALIA: MOUNTAINS	2
TOUR DE FRANCE: MOUNTAINS	2
VUELTA A ESPAÑA: MOUNTAINS	2
GRAND TOUR STAGE WINS	
RACE	POINTS
GIRO D'ITALIA	½ POINT
TOUR DE FRANCE	½ POINT
VUELTA A ESPAÑA	½ POINT

MASTER SCORING SHEET (CONTINUED)

SEASON-LONG COMPETITIONS	
RACE	POINTS
UNOFFICIAL SEASON LONG COMPETITION (PRE '48)	2
DESGRANGE-COLOMBO TROPHY ('48-'58)	2
SUPER PRESTIGE PERNOD TROPHY ('59-'87)	2
UCI ROAD WORLD CUP ('89-'04)	2
UCI ROAD WORLD ROAD RANKINGS ('84-'04)	2
UCI PROTOUR COMPETITION ('05-'08)	2
UCI WORLD TOUR ('09-PRESENT)	2
UCI WORLD RANKING ('16-PRESENT)	2

HOUR RECORD	
RACE	POINTS
HISTORICAL HOUR RECORD (PRE 1972)	3
UCI HOUR RECORD ('72-'14)	3
UCI UNIFIED HOUR RECORD ('14-PRESENT)	3

RACE RECORDS	
RACE	POINTS
MILAN SAN-REMO	3
TOUR OF FLANDERS	3
PARIS-ROUBAIX	4
LIÈGE-BASTOGNE-LIÈGE	3
IL LOMBARDIA/GIRO DI LOMBARDIA	3
GIRO D'ITALIA	6
TOUR DE FRANCE	8
VUELTA A ESPAÑA	5
WORLD CHAMPIONSHIP ROAD RACE	4

LIFETIME ACHIEVEMENTS	
RACE	POINTS
WON ALL FIVE MONUMENTS	15
25 COMBINED WINS IN ALL MAJOR SINGLE-DAY RACES	10
WON 30 GRAND TOUR STAGES	10
WON EIGHT GRAND TOURS	15
WON ALL THREE GRAND TOURS	10
WON ANY EIGHT GRAND TOUR CLASSIFICATION JERSEYS	10
ACHIEVED AT LEAST ONE VICTORY IN EVERY ROAD CATEGORY	10
WON 3 OF ANY 5 MONUMENTS AND ANY GRAND TOUR	10
WON 150 OR MORE PROFESSIONAL ROAD RACES	10

Rank 1: Eddy Merckx

BORN: **JUNE 17, 1945**
YEARS ACTIVE: **1965–1978**
COUNTRY: **BELGIUM**
NICKNAME: **THE CANNIBAL**

CAREER WINS: **292**
TOTAL POINTS: **418.50**
RAW SCORE: **294.5**

HE'S OBVIOUSLY THE WINNINGEST CYCLIST IN THE HISTORY OF THE SPORT, but if we were to divide those victories between one-day races and Grand Tours, he has more points than every other cyclist in *both* categories. He was the greatest single-day racer in the history of the sport, *and* he was the greatest Grand Tour cyclist in the history of the sport. Unreal. He not only won all five Monuments, but he is the only cyclist to have won all of them at least two times. He holds the record for most victories in both the Giro d'Italia (shared with Fausto Coppi) and Tour de France (shared with Jacques Anquetil, Bernard Hinault, and Miguel Induráin) at five apiece. He won the season-long competition, at the time called the Super Prestige Pernod Trophy, a record seven straight times. We will probably never bear witness to another seven-year run of dominance like that of Merckx from 1969 to 1975. It's a shame his name is not typically mentioned when discussing who might be the best athlete of all time (maybe that happens in Europe, but certainly not here in the United States). Based solely on his victories, he is undeniably the greatest in the history of the sport. From my perspective, there is absolutely no room for argument on this point—he is the only cyclist to own every single Career Milestone Adjustment in this scoring system. He truly was "The Cannibal." The shadow he's cast over the sport is so long that it was nearly impossible to complete the rest of these rider career highlights without his name constantly being referenced—Merckx is typically the benchmark for any type of special achievement.

RACE	POINTS	YEARS
THE MONUMENTS – 60 POINTS EARNED		
MILAN–SAN REMO:	3	1966, 1967, 1969, 1971, 1972, 1975, 1976
TOUR OF FLANDERS/RONDE VAN VLAANDEREN	3	1969, 1975
PARIS–ROUBAIX	4	1968, 1970, 1973
LIÈGE–BASTOGNE–LIÈGE	3	1969, 1971, 1972, 1973, 1975
IL LOMBARDIA/GIRO DI LOMBARDIA	3	1971, 1972
WORLD CHAMPIONSHIP ROAD RACE – 12 POINTS EARNED		
GOLD	4	1967, 1971, 1974
CLASSICS/OLYMPICS/TIME TRIALS – 18 POINTS EARNED		
GHENT–WEVELGEM	2	1967, 1970, 1973
AMSTEL GOLD	2	1973, 1975
LA FLÈCHE WALLONNE	2	1967, 1970, 1972
GRAND PRIX DE NATIONS	2	1973

ADDITIONAL EDDY MERCKX DATA CONTINUED ON THE NEXT PAGE...

RACE	POINTS	YEARS
SEMI-CLASSICS/NATIONALS – 17 POINTS EARNED		
BELGIAN NATIONAL RR CHAMPIONSHIPS	1	1970
OMLOOP HET NIEUWSBLAD/HET VOLK	1	1971, 1973
BRABANTSE PIJL/FLÈCHE BRABANÇONNE	1	1972
SCHELDEPRIJS/GP DE L'ESCAUT/GROTE SCHELDE-PRIJS/SCHELDEPRIJS VLAANDEREN	1	1972
ESCHBORN-FRANKFURT/FRANKFURT GRAND PRIX/RUND UM DEN HENNINGER-TURM	1	1971
BRUSSELS CYCLING CLASSIC/PARIS-BRUSSELS (POST 1966 EDITIONS)	1	1973
GRAND PRIX DE FOURMIES	1	1973
GIRO DELL'EMILIA	1	1972
TRE VALLE VARESINE	1	1968
GRAN PIEMONTE/GIRO DEL PIEMONTE	1	1972
CRITÉRIUM DES AS	1	1967, 1970, 1974
TROFEO BARACCHI	1	1966 (WITH FERDI BRACKE), 1967 (WITH FERDI BRACKE), 1972 (WITH ROGER SWERTS)
MINOR TOURS AND STAGE RACES – 39 POINTS EARNED		
PARIS-NICE	3	1969, 1970, 1971
VOLTA A CATALUNYA/TOUR OF CATALONIA	3	1968
TOUR OF ROMANDY	3	1968
CRITÉRIUM DU DAUPHINÉ/CRITÉRIUM DU DAU-PHINÉ LIBÉRÉ	3	1971
TOUR OF SWITZERLAND/TOUR DE SUISSE	3	1974
CATALAN WEEK/SETMANA CATALUNYA	2	1975, 1976
SETTIMANA INTERNAZIONALE COPPI E BARTALI/GIRO DI SARDEGNA	2	1968, 1971, 1973, 1975
TOUR OF BELGIUM	2	1970, 1971
GP MIDI LIBRE	2	1971

RACE	POINTS	YEARS
GRAND TOURS (VARIOUS POINTS) - 78 POINTS EARNED		
GIRO D'ITALIA		
1ST PLACE	6	1968, 1970, 1972, 1973, 1974
TOUR DE FRANCE		
1ST PLACE	8	1969, 1970, 1971, 1972, 1974
2ND PLACE	4	1975
VUELTA A ESPAÑA (TOUR OF SPAIN)		
1ST PLACE (PRE 1974)	4	1973
GRAND TOUR CLASSIFICATION JERSEYS - 18 POINTS EARNED		
GIRO D'ITALIA: POINTS	2	1968, 1973
TOUR DE FRANCE: POINTS	2	1969, 1971, 1972
VUELTA A ESPAÑA: POINTS	2	1973
GIRO D'ITALIA: MOUNTAINS	2	1968
TOUR DE FRANCE: MOUNTAINS	2	1969, 1970
GRAND TOUR STAGE WINS - 35.5 POINTS EARNED		
GIRO D'ITALIA: 25 STAGES	½ POINT	1968-1974
TOUR DE FRANCE: 34 STAGES (RACE RECORD), 6 TTT	½ POINT	1969-1977
VUELTA A ESPAÑA: 6 STAGES	½ POINT	1973
SEASON-LONG COMPETITIONS - 14 POINTS EARNED		
SUPER PRESTIGE PERNOD TROPHY	2	1969, 1970, 1971, 1972, 1973, 1974, 1975
HOUR RECORD - 3 POINTS EARNED		
UCI HOUR RECORD	3	1972

ADDITIONAL EDDY MERCKX DATA CONTINUED ON THE NEXT PAGE...

RACE RECORDS (VARIOUS POINTS) – 24 POINTS EARNED

MILAN SAN-REMO: 3 POINTS, EDDY MERCKX

LIÈGE-BASTOGNE-LIÈGE: 3 POINTS, EDDY MERCKX

GIRO D'ITALIA: 6 POINTS (SHARED WITH FAUSTO COPPI)

TOUR DE FRANCE: 8 POINTS (SHARED WITH JACQUES ANQUETIL, BERNARD HINAULT, AND MIGUEL INDURAIN)

WORLD CHAMPIONSHIP ROAD RACE: 4 POINTS (SHARED WITH ALFREDO BINDA, RIK VAN STEENBERGEN, OSCAR FREIRE, AND PETER SAGAN)

LIFETIME ACHIEVEMENTS (VARIOUS POINTS) – 100 POINTS EARNED

WON ALL FIVE MONUMENTS: 15 PTS

25 COMBINED WINS IN ALL MAJOR SINGLE-DAY RACES: 10 PTS

WON 30 GRAND TOUR STAGES: 10 PTS

WON EIGHT GRAND TOURS: 15 POINTS

WON ALL THREE GRAND TOURS: 10 POINTS

WON ANY EIGHT GRAND TOUR CLASSIFICATION JERSEYS: 10 POINTS

ACHIEVED AT LEAST ONE VICTORY IN EVERY ROAD CATEGORY: 10 POINTS

WON 3 OF ANY 5 MONUMENTS AND ANY GRAND TOUR: 10 POINTS

WON 150 OR MORE PROFESSIONAL ROAD RACES: 10 POINTS

1975 Amstel Gold Race Finish, Eddy Merckx (Right)

Rank 2: Bernard Hinault

BORN: **NOVEMBER 14, 1954**
YEARS ACTIVE: **1975–1986**
COUNTRY: **FRANCE**
NICKNAME:
LE BLAIREAU (THE BADGER),
LE PATRON (THE BOSS)

CAREER WINS: **149**
TOTAL POINTS: **232.5**
RAW SCORE: **169.5**

HINAULT IS FRANCE'S NUMBER ONE RANKED CYCLIST. He was the first to have won all three Grand Tours at least two times—three Giro, five Tours, and two Vuelta. Had it not been for a recurring knee injury in the middle of his career, I'm pretty sure he would have won the Tour a sixth time. The legendary *directeur sportif* Cyrille Guimard, whose riders included not only Hinault, but Lucien Van Impe, Laurent Fignon, and Greg LeMond, claimed that *Le Blaireau* (The Badger) was simply the strongest rider he'd ever witnessed. This coming from a man who rode alongside Merckx. In the 1981 edition of Paris-Roubaix, unbelievably still in the lead group after seven crashes, Hinault sped into the Roubaix velodrome to contest the final sprint with none other than Roger De Vlaeminck, Francesco Moser, Mark Demeyer, and Hennie Kuiper. Between them, those cyclists claimed an incredible ten Paris-Roubaix victories. Not only did "The Badger" win the sprint, but he actually led the group for the entire last lap—absolute domination. It could be argued that Hinault's victory in that edition of the race, against that legendary field, was one of the greatest sprint wins in the history of the sport. Maybe Guimard was correct; Hinault was the strongest ever. He turned pro in 1975 and took his time developing over the first couple of years by competing in many of the lesser-known races. That would change when he won the 1977 Ghent-Wevelgem, also winning Liège-Bastogne-Liège just five days later. His first Grand Tour was the 1978 Vuelta, which he won. He then went on to win his first Tour de France later that summer, earning the title of *Le Patron* (The Boss) when he represented the riders in their protest against the race organizers for continuing to schedule split stages (two stages raced in the same day). Hinault would command the respect of the peloton until his retirement in 1986, and it is fair to say that there hasn't been another badass boss of his kind since then.

RACE	POINTS	YEARS
THE MONUMENTS – 16 POINTS EARNED		
PARIS-ROUBAIX	4	1981
LIÈGE-BASTOGNE-LIÈGE	3	1977, 1980
IL LOMBARDIA/GIRO DI LOMBARDIA	3	1979, 1984
WORLD CHAMPIONSHIP ROAD RACE – 5 POINTS EARNED		
GOLD	4	1980
BRONZE	1	1981
CLASSICS/OLYMPICS/TIME TRIALS – 18 POINTS EARNED		
GHENT–WEVELGEM	2	1977
AMSTEL GOLD	2	1981
LA FLÈCHE WALLONNE	2	1979, 1983
GRAND PRIX DE NATIONS	2	1977, 1978, 1979, 1982, 1984

ADDITIONAL BERNARD HINAULT DATA CONTINUED ON THE NEXT PAGE...

RACE	POINTS	YEARS
SEMI-CLASSICS/NATIONALS – 3 POINTS EARNED		
FRENCH NATIONAL RR CHAMPIONSHIP	1	1978
CRITÉRIUM NATIONAL DE LA ROUTE		SERVED AS THE FRENCH NATIONAL ROAD RACE CHAMPIONSHIP IN 1978
CRITÉRIUM DES AS	1	1982
TROFEOANGELO BARACCHI	1	1984 (WITH FRANCESCO MOSER)
MINOR TOURS AND STAGE RACES – 18 POINTS EARNED		
TOUR OF ROMANDY	3	1980
CRITÉRIUM DU DAUPHINÉ/CRITÉRIUM DU DAU-PHINÉ LIBÉRÉ	3	1977, 1979, 1981
CRITÉRIUM INTERNATIONAL	2	1981
FOUR DAYS OF DUNKIRK	2	1984
TOUR DE LUXEMBOURG	2	1982
GRAND TOURS (VARIOUS POINTS) - 76 POINTS EARNED		
GIRO D'ITALIA		
1ST PLACE	6	1980, 1982, 1985
TOUR DE FRANCE		
1ST PLACE	8	1978, 1979, 1981, 1982, 1985
2ND PLACE	4	1984, 1986
VUELTA A ESPAÑA (TOUR OF SPAIN)		
1ST PLACE	5	1978, 1983
GRAND TOUR CLASSIFICATION JERSEYS – 4 POINTS EARNED		
TOUR DE FRANCE: POINTS	2	1979
TOUR DE FRANCE: MOUNTAINS	2	1986
GRAND TOUR STAGE WINS – 21.5 POINTS EARNED		
GIRO D'ITALIA: 7 STAGES, 1 TTT	½ POINT	1980, 1982, 1985
TOUR DE FRANCE: 29 STAGES, 1 TTT	½ POINT	1978-1986
VUELTA A ESPAÑA: 7 STAGES	½ POINT	1978, 1983

RACE	POINTS	YEARS
SEASON-LONG COMPETITIONS - 8 POINTS EARNED		
SUPER PRESTIGE PERNOD TROPHY	2	1979, 1980, 1981, 1982
RACE RECORDS (VARIOUS POINTS) - 8 POINTS EARNED		
TOUR DE FRANCE: 8 POINTS (SHARED WITH JACQUES ANQUETIL, EDDY MERCKX, AND MIGUEL INDURAIN)		
LIFETIME ACHIEVEMENTS (VARIOUS POINTS) - 55 POINTS EARNED		
WON 30 GRAND TOUR STAGES: 10 PTS		
WON EIGHT GRAND TOURS: 15 POINTS		
WON ALL THREE GRAND TOURS: 10 POINTS		
ACHIEVED AT LEAST ONE VICTORY IN EVERY ROAD CATEGORY: 10 POINTS		
WON 3 OF ANY 5 MONUMENTS AND ANY GRAND TOUR: 10 POINTS		

Rank 3: Fausto Coppi

BORN: **SEPTEMBER 15, 1919**
YEARS ACTIVE: **1939–1959**
COUNTRY: **ITALY**
NICKNAME:
THE HERON,
IL CAMPIONISSIMO
(THE CHAMPION OF CHAMPIONS)

CAREER WINS: **92**
TOTAL POINTS: **220.5**
RAW SCORE: **145.5**

ITALY'S TOP-RANKED CYCLIST. When *Il Campionissimo* (The Champion of Champions) was at his best and not recovering from one of his many broken bones, he was untouchable. Off the front for 147 kilometers in the 1946 Milan San Remo, Coppi won by an incredible fourteen minutes. He also won the 1952 Tour de France with a monstrous cushion of 28 minutes, 27 seconds—still the largest winning margin in the race's history. Once he got up the road alone, he was almost never caught. Coppi was also the first rider to accomplish the Giro/Tour double in the same year, 1949, a feat he duplicated in 1952. Coppi also set the hour record in 1942, which wouldn't be broken until 1956 by Jacques Anquetil. Coppi not only won a lot, but did so in style, perfection on the bike. In the words of his arch rival Gino Bartali, Coppi was "a god on a bicycle, fluid form in motion." I'm pretty sure Coppi would have surpassed Hinault's point totals had World War II not deprived him of five years of racing. *Il Campionissimo*, who had been coaching the team of Federico Bahamontes in 1959, went on a fateful hunting trip to Burkina Faso in December of that year. There he contracted a lethal strain of malaria from a mosquito bite. When he returned to Italy and fell ill, his doctors misdiagnosed his condition as the flu, and he deteriorated quickly; the fever that had gripped his body tragically claimed his life within days. He was only forty years old.

RACE	POINTS	YEARS
THE MONUMENTS – 28 POINTS EARNED		
MILAN–SAN REMO:	3	1946, 1948, 1949
PARIS-ROUBAIX	4	1950
IL LOMBARDIA/GIRO DI LOMBARDIA	3	1946, 1947, 1948, 1949, 1954
WORLD CHAMPIONSHIP ROAD RACE – 5 POINTS EARNED		
GOLD	4	1953
BRONZE	1	1949
CLASSICS/OLYMPICS/TIME TRIALS – 6 POINTS EARNED		
LA FLÈCHE WALLONNE	2	1950
GRAND PRIX DE NATIONS	2	1946, 1947
SEMI-CLASSICS/NATIONALS – 21 POINTS EARNED		
ITALIAN NATIONAL RR CHAMPIONSHIP	1	1942, 1947, 1949, 1955
GIRO DELLA ROMAGNA	1	1946, 1947, 1949
GIRO DELLA TOSCANA	1	1941
GIRO DELL'EMILIA	1	1941, 1947, 1948
TRE VALLE VARESINE	1	1941, 1948, 1955
GIRO DEL VENETO	1	1941, 1947, 1949
TROFEO BARACCHI	1	1953 (WITH RICCARDO FILIPPI), 1954 (WITH RICCARDO FILIPPI), 1955 (WITH RICCARDO FILIPPI, 1957 (WITH ERCOLE BALDINI)
MINOR TOURS AND STAGE RACES – 0 POINTS EARNED		

ADDITIONAL FAUSTO COPPI DATA CONTINUED ON THE NEXT PAGE...

RACE	POINTS	YEARS
GRAND TOURS (VARIOUS POINTS) - 52 POINTS EARNED		
GIRO D'ITALIA		
IST PLACE	6	1940, 1947, 1949, 1952, 1953
2ND PLACE	3	1946, 1955
TOUR DE FRANCE		
IST PLACE	8	1949, 1952
GRAND TOUR CLASSIFICATION JERSEYS – 10 POINTS EARNED		
GIRO D'ITALIA: MOUNTAINS	2	1948, 1949, 1954
TOUR DE FRANCE: MOUNTAINS	2	1949, 1952
GRAND TOUR STAGE WINS - 16.5 POINTS EARNED		
GIRO D'ITALIA: 22 STAGES	½ POINT	1940-1955
TOUR DE FRANCE: 9 STAGES, 2 TTT	½ POINT	1949-1954
SEASON-LONG COMPETITIONS – 4 POINTS EARNED		
UNOFFICIAL SEASON LONG COMPETITION	2	1946
DESGRANGE-COLOMBO TROPHY	2	1949
HOUR RECORD - 3 POINTS EARNED		
HISTORICAL HOUR RECORD	3	1942
RACE RECORDS (VARIOUS POINTS) – 9 POINTS EARNED		
IL LOMBARDIA/GIRO DI LOMBARDIA: 3 POINTS		
GIRO D'ITALIA: 6 POINTS (SHARED WITH EDDY MERCKX)		
LIFETIME ACHIEVEMENTS (VARIOUS POINTS) – 66 POINTS EARNED		
25 COMBINED WINS IN ALL MAJOR SINGLE-DAY RACES: 10 PTS		
WON 30 GRAND TOUR STAGES: 10 PTS		
WON 3 OF ANY 5 MONUMENTS AND ANY GRAND TOUR: 10 POINTS		
MISSING YEARS ADJUSTMENT: 36 POINTS		

Rank 4: Gino Bartali

BORN: **JULY 18, 1914**
YEARS ACTIVE: **1935–1954**
COUNTRY: **ITALY**
NICKNAME:
GINO THE PIOUS / GENETACCIO
L'UOMO DI FERRO
(THE MAN OF STEEL)

CAREER WINS: **87**
TOTAL POINTS: **213**
RAW SCORE: **144.5**

BACK IN PART II OF THIS BOOK, in the section titled "Gino and Fausto," I elaborated on why I felt Bartali was the cyclist who would have perhaps been closest to Merckx in career victories had World War II not erased his prime years. Rarely does his name come up when discussing the great climbers of the sport, yet he won seven mountain classifications between the Giro and the Tour; again, this despite missing five years of opportunities to add to that number during the peak of his career. The longstanding argument of who was Italy's greatest cyclist, Bartali or Coppi, is not really answered by this ranking system; they are only separated by a single point in their raw scores, with Fausto just edging out Gino. It's interesting that after Coppi, the largest winning margin in the Tour de France belongs to Gino — "The Man of Iron" claimed a 26 minute, 16 second buffer over second-place Briek Schotte in the 1948 race. That is also the same Tour in which Gino set the still-standing record of the longest interval in between victories—ten years, as his last win in the French GT had been back in 1938. No mention of "Gino the Pious" would be complete without recognizing his humanitarian acts during the war years—protecting and aiding the Jewish community in Italy. It is those efforts that have recently shed light on his greater significance outside the sporting world. For those wanting to learn more about this fascinating story, I would suggest reading *Road to Valour* by Aili and Andres McConnon; you will come away with a much deeper appreciation of one of the legends, and great humans, of this sport.

RACE	POINTS	YEARS
THE MONUMENTS – 21 POINTS EARNED		
MILAN-SAN REMO:	3	1939, 1940, 1947, 1950
IL LOMBARDIA/GIRO DI LOMBARDIA	3	1936, 1939, 1940
WORLD CHAMPIONSHIP ROAD RACE – 0 POINTS EARNED		
CLASSICS/OLYMPICS/TIME TRIALS – 4 POINTS EARNED		
CHAMPIONSHIP OF ZURICH/ZÜRI-METZGETE	2	1946, 1948
SEMI-CLASSICS/NATIONALS – 17 POINTS EARNED		
ITALIAN NATIONAL RR CHAMPIONSHIP	1	1935, 1940, 1952
GIRO DEL LAZIO	1	1937, 1940, 1945
GIRO DELLA TOSCANA	1	1939, 1940, 1948, 1950, 1953
GIRO DELL'EMILIA	1	1952, 1953
TRE VALLE VARESINE	1	1938
GRAN PIEMONTE/GIRO DEL PIEMONTE	1	1937, 1939, 1951
MINOR TOURS AND STAGE RACES – 12 POINTS EARNED		
TOUR OF THE BASQUE COUNTRY/VUELTA CICLISTA AL PAIS VASCO	3	1935
TOUR OF ROMANDY	3	1949
TOUR OF SWITZERLAND/TOUR DE SUISSE	3	1946, 1947

ADDITIONAL GINO BARTALI DATA CONTINUED ON THE NEXT PAGE...

RACE	POINTS	YEARS
GRAND TOURS (VARIOUS POINTS) - 50 POINTS EARNED		
GIRO D'ITALIA		
IST PLACE	6	1936, 1937, 1946
2ND PLACE	3	1939, 1947, 1949, 1950
TOUR DE FRANCE		
IST PLACE	8	1938, 1948
2ND PLACE	4	1949
GRAND TOUR CLASSIFICATION JERSEYS – 18 POINTS EARNED		
GIRO D'ITALIA: MOUNTAINS	2	1935, 1936, 1937, 1939, 1940, 1946, 1947
TOUR DE FRANCE: MOUNTAINS	2	1938, 1948
GRAND TOUR STAGE WINS – 14.5 POINTS EARNED		
GIRO D'ITALIA: 17 STAGES	½ POINT	1935-1954
TOUR DE FRANCE: 12 STAGES	½ POINT	1937-1950
SEASON-LONG COMPETITIONS – 8 POINTS EARNED		
UNOFFICIAL SEASON LONG COMPETITION (PRE '48)	2	1936, 1937, 1939, 1947
HOUR RECORD - 0 POINTS EARNED		
RACE RECORDS (VARIOUS POINTS) – 0 POINTS EARNED		
LIFETIME ACHIEVEMENTS (VARIOUS POINTS) – 68.5 POINTS EARNED		
25 COMBINED WINS IN ALL MAJOR SINGLE-DAY RACES: 10 PTS		
WON ANY EIGHT GRAND TOUR CLASSIFICATION JERSEYS: 10 POINTS		
MISSING YEARS ADJUSTMENT: 48.5		

Rank 5: Jacques Anquetil

BORN: **JANUARY 18, 1934**
YEARS ACTIVE: **1954–1969**
COUNTRY: **FRANCE**
NICKNAME:
MONSIEUR CHRONO (MR. TIME),
MAÎTRE JACQUES
(MASTER JACQUES)

CAREER WINS: **132**
TOTAL POINTS: **191.5**
RAW SCORE: **158.5**

Monsieur Chrono (Mr. Time) and *Maître Jacques* (Master Jacques)—it is the first of those two famous nicknames that solidifies his pecking order on this list. He is the first non-all-rounder to make this list; a specialist in time trials and stage races. Had it not been for his victory in the 1966 Liège-Bastogne-Liège, in the twilight of his career, he'd have been the only cyclist to have made the Top 10 without a victory in a Monument—all others in the Top 10 had at least four of them. In contrast to this dearth of single-day Classic triumphs, Anquetil captured nine victories in the world time trial championships at the time, the Grand Prix de Nations, six of those in consecutive years. This prodigious time trial ability was also fundamental to Anquetil's eight Grand Tour victories—all but three of his twenty-two stage wins were in time trials. This gift against the clock helped him secure five Tours, two Giro, and a Vuelta; he was the first to win all three Grand Tours. Along with Coppi, Merckx, and Bradley Wiggins, Anquetil is the only other cyclist in the Top 100 to have held the official UCI hour record.

RACE	POINTS	YEARS
THE MONUMENTS – 3 POINTS EARNED		
LIÈGE–BASTOGNE–LIÈGE	3	1966
WORLD CHAMPIONSHIP ROAD RACE – 2 POINTS EARNED		
SILVER	2	1966
CLASSICS/OLYMPICS/TIME TRIALS – 22 POINTS EARNED		
GHENT–WEVELGEM	2	1964
BORDEAUX–PARIS	2	1965
GRAND PRIX DE NATIONS	2	1953, 1954, 1955, 1956, 1957, 1958, 1961, 1965, 1966
SEMI-CLASSICS/NATIONALS – 11 POINTS EARNED		
FRENCH NATIONAL RR CHAMPIONSHIP	1	1961, 1963, 1965, 1967
CRITÉRIUM NATIONAL DE LA ROUTE		SERVED AS THE FRENCH NATIONAL RR CHAMPIONSHIP
CRITÉRIUM DES AS	1	1959, 1960, 1963, 1965
TROFEO BARACCHI	1	1962 (WITH RUDI ALTIG), 1965 (WITH JEAN STA-BLINSKI), 1968 (WITH FELICE GIMONDI)
MINOR TOURS AND STAGE RACES – 35 POINTS EARNED		
PARIS–NICE	3	1957, 1961, 1963, 1965, 1966
VOLTA A CATALUNYA/TOUR OF CATALONIA	3	1967
TOUR OF THE BASQUE COUNTRY/VUELTA CICLISTA AL PAIS VASCO	3	1969
CRITÉRIUM DU DAUPHINÉ/CRITÉRIUM DU DAUPHINÉ LIBÉRÉ	3	1963, 1965
SETTIMANA INTERNAZIONALE COPPI E BARTALI/GIRO DI SARDEGNA	2	1966
FOUR DAYS OF DUNKIRK	2	1958, 1959, 1960

ADDITIONAL JACQUES ANQUETIL DATA CONTINUED ON THE NEXT PAGE...

RACE	POINTS	YEARS
GRAND TOURS (VARIOUS POINTS) - 63 POINTS EARNED		
GIRO D'ITALIA		
IST PLACE	6	1960, 1964
2ND PLACE	3	1959
3RD PLACE	I	1966, 1967
TOUR DE FRANCE		
IST PLACE	8	1957, 1961, 1962, 1963, 1964
3RD PLACE	2	1959
VUELTA A ESPAÑA (TOUR OF SPAIN)		
IST PLACE (PRE 1974)	4	1963
GRAND TOUR CLASSIFICATION JERSEYS – 0 POINTS EARNED		
GRAND TOUR STAGE WINS - 11.5 POINTS EARNED		
GIRO D'ITALIA: 5 STAGES	½ POINT	1959-1964
TOUR DE FRANCE: 16 STAGES, 1 TTT	½ POINT	1957-1964
VUELTA A ESPAÑA: 1 STAGE	½ POINT	1963
SEASON-LONG COMPETITIONS – 8 POINTS EARNED		
SUPER PRESTIGE PERNOD TROPHY	2	1961, 1963, 1965, 1966
HOUR RECORD - 3 POINTS EARNED		
HISTORICAL HOUR RECORD	3	1956
RACE RECORDS (VARIOUS POINTS) – 8 POINTS EARNED		
TOUR DE FRANCE: 8 POINTS (SHARED WITH EDDY MERCKX, BERNARD HINAULT, AND MIGUEL INDURÁIN)		
LIFETIME ACHIEVEMENTS (VARIOUS POINTS) – 25 POINTS EARNED		
WON EIGHT GRAND TOURS: 15 POINTS		
WON ALL THREE GRAND TOURS: 10 POINTS		

Rank 6: Sean Kelly

BORN: **MAY 24, 1956**
YEARS ACTIVE: **1977-1994**
COUNTRY: **IRELAND**
NICKNAME: **KING KELLY**

CAREER WINS: **160**
TOTAL POINTS: **169.5**
RAW SCORE: **139.5**

IRELAND'S GREATEST CYCLIST. Although Kelly is usually remembered as one of the best single-day racers of all time, he was also an amazing stage racer. In fact, Kelly was the greatest Minor Tour rider in the history of the sport. Yes, he even scored more points than Merckx; this statistic complements of his seven consecutive victories in Paris-Nice, from 1982 to 1988. His other weeklong stage race victories included the Tour of Switzerland, the Volta a Catalunya, the Tour of the Basque Country, and the Setmana Catalana. Although not a weeklong stage race, he also won three editions of the Critérium International. Kelly also won a Grand Tour, the 1988 Tour of Spain, and also claimed four points classifications in both the Tour and Vuelta. If the Irish hardman had been just a wee bit more of a *grimpeur** than a *rouleur*, I'm pretty sure he would have been right up there with Coppi and Bartali in point totals. Kelly was certainly a capable climber, as he finished in the top ten eight times in both the Tour and Vuelta. So, yes, he had great success as a stage racer, but he also won four of the five Monuments—nine

---

Grimpeur is French for climber, while rouleur is French for a cyclist who excels on flat and rolling terrain.

in total—so he was also quite the single-day monster. "King Kelly" also won nine season-long competitions, the most in the history of the sport, one of the few records Merckx doesn't own. I'd be willing to bet he'd trade one of those honors for that missing World Championship Road Race title. Perhaps he'd even trade another for the one Monument missing from his *palmarès*—the Tour of Flanders. The case can certainly be made that once Kelly retired in 1994, the end of an era had arrived. With rare exceptions, gone were the days of the true all-rounder, cyclists who raced for victory from the beginning of the season to the end and would play their hand in any type of race. The age of the specialist had arrived, and cycling has been the poorer for it ever since.

RACE	POINTS	YEARS
THE MONUMENTS – 29 POINTS EARNED		
MILAN–SAN REMO:	3	1986, 1992
PARIS–ROUBAIX	4	1984, 1986
LIÈGE–BASTOGNE–LIÈGE	3	1984, 1989
IL LOMBARDIA/GIRO DI LOMBARDIA	3	1983, 1985, 1991
WORLD CHAMPIONSHIP ROAD RACE – 2 POINTS EARNED		
BRONZE	1	1982, 1989
CLASSICS/OLYMPICS/TIME TRIALS – 4 POINTS EARNED		
GHENT–WEVELGEM	2	1988
GRAND PRIX DE NATIONS	2	1986
SEMI-CLASSICS/NATIONALS – 4 POINTS EARNED		
BRETAGNE CLASSIC OUEST–FRANCE/GP OUEST–FRANCE/GRAND PRIX DE PLOUAY	1	1984
CRITÉRIUM DES AS	1	1984, 1985, 1986

ADDITIONAL SEAN KELLY DATA CONTINUED ON THE NEXT PAGE...

RACE	POINTS	YEARS
MINOR TOURS AND STAGE RACES – 50 POINTS EARNED		
PARIS-NICE	3	1982, 1983, 1984, 1985, 1986, 1987, 1988
VOLTA A CATALUNYA/TOUR OF CATALONIA	3	1984, 1986
TOUR OF THE BASQUE COUNTRY/VUELTA CICLISTA AL PAIS VASCO	3	1984, 1986, 1987
TOUR OF SWITZERLAND/TOUR DE SUISSE	3	1983, 1990
CRITÉRIUM INTERNATIONAL	2	1983, 1984, 1987
CATALAN WEEK/SETMANA CATALUNYA	2	1988
GRAND TOURS (VARIOUS POINTS) - 6 POINTS EARNED		
VUELTA A ESPAÑA (TOUR OF SPAIN)		
1ST PLACE	5	1988
3RD PLACE	1	1986
GRAND TOUR CLASSIFICATION JERSEYS – 16 POINTS EARNED		
TOUR DE FRANCE: POINTS	2	1982, 1983, 1985, 1989
VUELTA A ESPAÑA: POINTS	2	1980, 1985, 1986, 1988
GRAND TOUR STAGE WINS – 10.5 POINTS EARNED		
TOUR DE FRANCE: 5 STAGES	½ POINT	1978-1982
VUELTA A ESPAÑA: 16 STAGES	½ POINT	1979-1988
SEASON-LONG COMPETITIONS – 18 POINTS EARNED		
SUPER PRESTIGE PERNOD TROPHY	2	1984, 1985, 1986
UCI ROAD WORLD CUP	2	1989
UCI ROAD WORLD ROAD RANKINGS	2	1984, 1985, 1986, 1987, 1988
HOUR RECORD - 0 POINTS EARNED		
RACE RECORDS (VARIOUS POINTS) – 0 POINTS EARNED		
LIFETIME ACHIEVEMENTS (VARIOUS POINTS) – 30 POINTS EARNED		
WON ANY EIGHT GRAND TOUR CLASSIFICATION JERSEYS: 10 POINTS		
WON 3 OF ANY 5 MONUMENTS AND ANY GRAND TOUR: 10 POINTS		
WON 150 OR MORE PROFESSIONAL ROAD RACES: 10 POINTS		

Rank 7: Francesco Moser

BORN: **JUNE 19, 1951**
YEARS ACTIVE: **1973-1988**
COUNTRY: **ITALY**
NICKNAME: *CHECCO* ,
LO SCERIFFO (THE SHERIFF)

CAREER WINS: **152**
TOTAL POINTS: **156.5**
RAW SCORE: **116.5**

Lo Sceriffo (The Sheriff) won more Semi-Classics than every other cyclist on this list, was World Champion in 1977, won three straight Paris-Roubaix, captured three of the five Monuments, was victorious in four other Classics, won a Giro and four of its points classifications, racked up twenty-seven wins in Grand Tour stages, and captured a Super Prestige Pernod Trophy. Although not a true climber, he was a ferocious competitor and did manage to win the 1984 Giro. He would also place second in that race three times and third twice. *Cecco* also claimed six Minor Tours. He was a true all-rounder, cast from the same mold as legends of the past like Coppi and Bartali, and like those two, he also had an arch rival Italian counterpart in Giuseppe Saronni. Moser was also a great time trialist, and nearly half of his GT wins came in either prologues or time trials. He did break the hour record in 1984, but under the newer UCI guidelines established in 1997, that record was later moved to the Best Human Effort category, not the official UCI hour record.

RACE	POINTS	YEARS
THE MONUMENTS – 21 POINTS EARNED		
MILAN–SAN REMO:	3	1984
PARIS–ROUBAIX	4	1978, 1979, 1980
IL LOMBARDIA/GIRO DI LOMBARDIA	3	1975, 1978
WORLD CHAMPIONSHIP ROAD RACE - 8 POINTS EARNED		
GOLD	4	1977
SILVER	2	1976, 1978
CLASSICS/OLYMPICS/TIME TRIALS – 8 POINTS EARNED		
GHENT–WEVELGEM	2	1979
LA FLÈCHE WALLONNE	2	1977
PARIS–TOURS	2	1974
CHAMPIONSHIP OF ZURICH/ZURI-METZGETE	2	1977
SEMI-CLASSICS/NATIONALS – 24 POINTS EARNED		
ITALIAN NATIONAL RR CHAMPIONSHIPS	1	1975, 1979, 1981
GIRO DEL LAZIO	1	1977,1978, 1984
GIRO DELLA TOSCANA	1	1974, 1976, 1977, 1982
MILANO-TORINO/MILAN-TURIN	1	1983
GIRO DELL'EMILIA	1	1974, 1979
TRE VALLE VARESINE	1	1976,1978
GRAN PIEMONTE/GIRO DEL PIEMONTE	1	1974
COPPA PLACCI	1	1975
GIRO DEL VENETO	1	1979
CRITÉRIUM DES AS	1	1977
TROFEO BARACCHI	1	1974 (WITH ROY SCHUITEN), 1975 (WITH GIANBATTISTA BARONCHELLI), 1979 (WITH GIUSEPPE SARONNI), 1984 (WITH BERNARD HINAULT), 1985 (WITH HANS-HENRIK ORSTED)

ADDITIONAL FRANCESCO MOSER CONTINUED ON THE NEXT PAGE...

RACE	POINTS	YEARS
MINOR TOURS AND STAGE RACES – 15 POINTS EARNED		
TIRRENO–ADRIATICO	3	1980, 1981
VOLTA A CATALUNYA/TOUR OF CATALONIA	3	1978
TOUR OF THE ALPS/GIRO DEL TRENTINO	2	1980, 1983
GP MIDI LIBRE	2	1975
GRAND TOURS (VARIOUS POINTS) - 17 POINTS EARNED		
GIRO D'ITALIA		
IST PLACE	6	1984
2ND PLACE	3	1977, 1979, 1985
3RD PLACE	I	1978, 1986
GRAND TOUR CLASSIFICATION JERSEYS – 8 POINTS EARNED		
GIRO D'ITALIA: POINTS	2	1976, 1977, 1978, 1982
GRAND TOUR STAGE WINS – 13.5 POINTS EARNED		
GIRO D'ITALIA: 23 STAGES	½ POINT	1973–1986
TOUR DE FRANCE: 2 STAGES	½ POINT	1975
VUELTA A ESPAÑA: 2 STAGES	½ POINT	1984
SEASON-LONG COMPETITIONS – 2 POINTS EARNED		
SUPER PRESTIGE PERNOD TROPHY	2	1978
HOUR RECORD - 0 POINTS EARNED		
RACE RECORDS (VARIOUS POINTS) – 0 POINTS EARNED		
LIFETIME ACHIEVEMENTS (VARIOUS POINTS) – 40 POINTS EARNED		
25 COMBINED WINS IN ALL MAJOR SINGLE-DAY RACES: 10 PTS		
ACHIEVED AT LEAST ONE VICTORY IN EVERY ROAD CATEGORY: 10 POINTS		
WON 3 OF ANY 5 MONUMENTS AND ANY GRAND TOUR: 10 POINTS		
WON 150 OR MORE PROFESSIONAL ROAD RACES: 10 POINTS		

Rank 8: Roger De Vlaeminck

BORN: **AUGUST 24, 1947**
YEARS ACTIVE: **1969-1984**
COUNTRY: **BELGIUM**
NICKNAME: **THE GYPSY,
MR. PARIS-ROUBAIX**

CAREER WINS: **165**
TOTAL POINTS: **152**
RAW SCORE: **114**

IT IS ONLY ROGER DE VLAEMINCK, MERCKX, AND RIK VAN LOOY
WHO WERE ABLE TO WIN ALL FIVE MONUMENTS. After Merckx, I'd
give the nod to De Vlaeminck as the greatest Classics specialist on
this list. Yes, Van Looy actually had more Classics victories, but
De Vlaeminck won more Monuments, and after Moser, he and
Coppi had more Semi-Classic victories than any others. Along with
Tom Boonen, he captured the most Paris-Roubaix victories—four,
thus earning one of his nicknames, "Mr. Paris-Roubaix." What is
remarkable about many of those victories is that they were achieved
during Merckx's amazing seven-year run of domination from 1969 to
1975, which goes to show that "The Cannibal" didn't necessarily win
everything. De Vlaeminck was still racking up big wins later in the
1970s, but by then was vying for victory with such greats as Freddy
Maertens, Francesco Moser, Jan Raas, and Bernard Hinault. It's hard
to believe that he never won a season-long competition, but at the
time he competed nearly all the other cyclists who were also in the
running for the Super Prestige Pernod Trophy were also successful
Grand Tour riders, which was the one type of race in which De
Vlaeminck was never a factor. Like Sean Kelly, he's another cyclist

who I'd bet would be willing to trade one his significant victories for that elusive World Championship RR title. He did come close on many occasions, but I'm wondering just how many times he was actually the designated team leader. It's too bad points weren't issued in this system for looking like a cycling god, having a nickname like "The Gypsy," sporting epic '70s-era sideburns, and rocking one of the most iconic cycling kits to ever grace the peloton.* Had that been the case, then De Vlaeminck would certainly have scooped up a Career Milestone Adjustment in the style category, offsetting the points he didn't get from the missing WC gold medal.

Brooklyn Chewing Gum was the sponsor of De Vlaeminck's team from 1973–1977. Although named after the bridge in New York, with very American corporate branding and team kits featuring a red, white, and blue design, the company was actually Italian. They are still in business and have been a staple in Italy since the 1950s.

RACE	POINTS	YEARS
THE MONUMENTS – 37 POINTS EARNED		
MILAN–SAN REMO:	3	1973, 1978, 1979
TOUR OF FLANDERS/RONDE VAN VLAANDEREN	3	1977
PARIS-ROUBAIX	4	1972, 1974, 1975, 1977
LIÈGE-BASTOGNE-LIÈGE	3	1970
IL LOMBARDIA/GIRO DI LOMBARDIA	3	1974, 1976
WORLD CHAMPIONSHIP ROAD RACE – 2 POINTS EARNED		
SILVER	2	1975
CLASSICS/OLYMPICS/TIME TRIALS – 4 POINTS EARNED		
LA FLÈCHE WALLONNE	2	1971
CHAMPIONSHIP OF ZURICH/ZÜRI-METZGETE	2	1975

ADDITIONAL ROGER DE VLAEMINCK CONTINUED ON THE NEXT PAGE...

RACE	POINTS	YEARS
SEMI-CLASSICS/NATIONALS – 21 POINTS EARNED		
BELGIAN NATIONAL RR CHAMPIONSHIPS	1	1969, 1981
OMLOOP HET NIEUWSBLAD/HET VOLK	1	1969, 1979
KUURNE–BRUSSELS–KUURNE	1	1970, 1971
GIRO DEL LAZIO	1	1975, 1976
E3 BINKBANK CLASSIC/E3 HARELBEKE/HARELBEKE–ANTWERP–HARELBEKE/E3 PRIJS VLAANDEREN	1	1971
BRABANTSE PIJL	1	1981
SCHELDEPRIJS/GP DE L'ESCAUT/GROTE SCHELDEPRIJS/SCHELDEPRIJS VLAANDEREN	1	1970
BRUSSELS CYCLING CLASSIC/PARIS-BRUSSELS	1	1981
GIRO DELLA TOSCANA	1	1973
MILANO-TORINO/MILAN-TURIN	1	1972, 1974
GIRO DELL'EMILIA	1	1976
GRAN PIEMONTE/GIRO DEL PIEMONTE	1	1977
COPPA PLACCI	1	1972, 1974
GIRO DEL VENETO	1	1974
CRITÉRIUM DES AS	1	1975
MINOR TOURS AND STAGE RACES – 32 POINTS EARNED		
TIRRENO–ADRIATICO	3	1972, 1973, 1974, 1975, 1976, 1977
VOLTA A CATALUNYA/TOUR OF CATALONIA	3	1976
TOUR OF SWITZERLAND/TOUR DE SUISSE	3	1975
FOUR DAYS OF DUNKIRK	2	1971
SETTIMANA INTERNAZIONALE COPPI E BARTALI/GIRO DI SARDEGNA	2	1976, 1978, 1980
GRAND TOURS (VARIOUS POINTS) – 0 POINTS EARNED		

RACE	POINTS	YEARS
GRAND TOUR CLASSIFICATION JERSEYS – 6 POINTS EARNED		
VUELTA A ESPAÑA: POINTS	2	1972, 1974, 1975
GRAND TOUR STAGE WINS - 12 POINTS EARNED		
GIRO D'ITALIA: 22 STAGES	½ POINT	1972–1979
TOUR DE FRANCE: 1 STAGE	½ POINT	1970
VUELTA A ESPAÑA: 1 STAGE	½ POINT	1984
SEASON-LONG COMPETITIONS – 0 POINTS EARNED		
HOUR RECORD - 0 POINTS EARNED		
RACE RECORDS (VARIOUS POINTS) – 4 POINTS EARNED		
PARIS-ROUBAIX: 4 POINTS (SHARED WITH TOM BOONEN)		
LIFETIME ACHIEVEMENTS (VARIOUS POINTS) – 35 POINTS EARNED		
WON ALL FIVE MONUMENTS: 15 PTS		
25 COMBINED WINS IN ALL MAJOR SINGLE-DAY RACES: 10 PTS		
WON 150 OR MORE PROFESSIONAL ROAD RACES: 10 POINTS		

Rank 9: Rik Van Looy

BORN: **DECEMBER 20, 1933**
YEARS ACTIVE: **1953–1970**
COUNTRY: **BELGIUM**
NICKNAME: **RIK II,**
KEISER VAN HERENTALS
(THE EMPEROR OF HERENTALS)

CAREER WINS: **165**
TOTAL POINTS: **152**
RAW SCORE: **107**

VAN LOOY'S WINS CAME PRIMARILY IN SINGLE-DAY RACES; after all, he was known as "King of the Classics." He was twice the World Road Race champion, in 1960 and '61, and placed second in 1956 and '63. Van Looy, along with Merckx and Roger De Vlaeminck, is the only other cyclist to have won all five Monuments. Yet, despite those successes in the greatest of the one-day races, he also managed to make the third step of the podium in the 1959 and 1965 Vuelta. It's no surprise that Van Looy won the points competition in the Tour and Vuelta three times, but as a testament to his overall capabilities, he also won the mountains classification in the 1960 Giro. Unbelievably, both Van Looy and Merckx were on the same team in '65, a situation that was for obvious reasons short-lived.

RACE	POINTS	YEARS
THE MONUMENTS - 27 POINTS EARNED		
MILAN–SAN REMO:	3	1958
TOUR OF FLANDERS/RONDE VAN VLAANDEREN	3	1959, 1962
PARIS–ROUBAIX	4	1961, 1962, 1965
LIÈGE–BASTOGNE–LIÈGE	3	1961
IL LOMBARDIA/GIRO DI LOMBARDIA	3	1959
WORLD CHAMPIONSHIP ROAD RACE - 12 POINTS EARNED		
GOLD	4	1960, 1961
SILVER	2	1956, 1963
CLASSICS/OLYMPICS/TIME TRIALS - 16 POINTS EARNED		
GHENT–WEVELGEM	2	1956, 1957, 1962
LA FLÈCHE WALLONNE	2	1968
PARIS–TOURS	2	1959, 1967
PARIS–BRUSSELS	2	1956, 1958
SEMI-CLASSICS/NATIONALS - 9 POINTS EARNED		
BELGIAN NATIONAL RR CHAMPIONSHIPS	1	1958, 1963
E3 BINKBANK CLASSIC/E3 HARELBEKE/HARELBEKE–ANTWERP–HARELBEKE/E3 PRIJS VLAANDEREN	1	1964, 1965, 1966, 1969
SCHELDEPRIJS/GP DE L'ESCAUT/GROTE SCHELDEPRIJS/SCHELDEPRIJS VLAANDEREN	1	1956, 1957
CRITÉRIUM DES AS	1	1961
MINOR TOURS AND STAGE RACES - 12 POINTS EARNED		
SETTIMANA INTERNAZIONALE COPPI E BARTALI/GIRO DI SARDEGNA	2	1959, 1962, 1965
TOUR OF BELGIUM	2	1961
BINCKBANK TOUR/ENECO TOUR OF BENELUX/RONDE VAN NEDERLANDS	2	1956, 1957
GRAND TOURS (VARIOUS POINTS) - 2 POINTS EARNED		
VUELTA A ESPAÑA (TOUR OF SPAIN)		
3RD PLACE	1	1959, 1965

ADDITIONAL RIK VAN LOOY CONTINUED ON THE NEXT PAGE...

RACE	POINTS	YEARS
GRAND TOUR CLASSIFICATION JERSEYS – 8 POINTS EARNED		
TOUR DE FRANCE: POINTS	2	1963
VUELTA A ESPAÑA: POINTS	2	1959,1965
GIRO D'ITALIA: MOUNTAINS	2	1960
GRAND TOUR STAGE WINS – 19 POINTS EARNED		
GIRO D'ITALIA: 12 STAGES	½ POINT	1959-1962
TOUR DE FRANCE: 7 STAGES, 1 TTT	½ POINT	1963-1969
VUELTA A ESPAÑA: 18 STAGES	½ POINT	1958-1965
SEASON-LONG COMPETITIONS – 2 POINTS EARNED		
SUPER PRESTIGE PERNOD TROPHY	2	1959
HOUR RECORD – 0 POINTS EARNED		
RACE RECORDS (VARIOUS POINTS) – 0 POINTS EARNED		
LIFETIME ACHIEVEMENTS (VARIOUS POINTS) – 45 POINTS EARNED		
WON ALL FIVE MONUMENTS: 15 PTS		
25 COMBINED WINS IN ALL MAJOR SINGLE-DAY RACES: 10 PTS		
WON 30 GRAND TOUR STAGES: 10 PTS		
WON 150 OR MORE PROFESSIONAL ROAD RACES: 10 POINTS		

Rank 10: Alejandro Valverde

BORN: **APRIL 24, 1980**
YEARS ACTIVE: **2002-PRESENT**
COUNTRY: **SPAIN**
NICKNAME: *BALAVERDE*
(THE GREEN BULLET) /
EL IMBATIDO (THE UNBEATEN)

CAREER WINS: **129**
TOTAL POINTS: **115**
RAW SCORE: **105**

THE POINTS VALVERDE EARNED IN THE 2019 SEASON were enough to overtake Miguel Induráin and he is now Spain's top ranked cyclist. When Valverde crashed in the 2017 Tour de France and fractured his kneecap, I was pretty sure he was done. After all, he was thirty-seven at the time and had already had a rather illustrious career. Despite serving a two-year ban for a doping violation—his 2010 results were annulled and he didn't compete in 2011—he ended the 2017 season with enough points to occupy the nineteenth spot in these rankings. His *palmarès* up to that point were certainly impressive, but *Balaverde* (The Green Bullet) had unfinished business in the World Championship Road Race. He'd reached the podium more times than any other cyclist—two silver and four bronze medals—but the top step of the podium had always eluded him. So, he returned from his potentially career-ending injury, a man on a mission, and had one of his best seasons ever.

By the end of 2018, Valverde had not only captured that elusive WC gold medal, but also sat atop the UCI World Rankings. Ten of Valverde's massive twenty-two points earned in 2018 came from the rare accomplishment of winning a race in every category in this scoring system. He is now one of only seven cyclists to join this exclusive club of the best all-rounders who have competed in the Modern Era—Louison Bobet, Ferdi Kübler, Jan Janssen, Eddy Merckx, Francesco Moser, and Bernard Hinault.

As a testament to his amazing consistency, the Spaniard has placed in the top ten in 19 Grand Tours. In this era of specialization, it's the rare cyclist who competes all season long in a variety of races and can win almost anything. At the time of this writing, the thirty-nine-year-old Valverde is still going strong and has signed on with his Movistar team through the 2021 season.

RACE	POINTS	YEARS
THE MONUMENTS – 12 POINTS EARNED		
LIÈGE-BASTOGNE-LIÈGE	3	2006, 2008, 2015, 2017
WORLD CHAMPIONSHIP ROAD RACE - 12 POINTS EARNED		
GOLD	4	2018
SILVER	2	2003, 2005
BRONZE	1	2006, 2012, 2013, 2014
CLASSICS/OLYMPICS/TIME TRIALS – 14 POINTS EARNED		
LA FLÈCHE WALLONNE	2	2006, 2014, 2015, 2016, 2017
CLÁSICA DE SAN SEBASTIÁN	2	2008, 2014
SEMI-CLASSICS/NATIONALS – 4 POINTS EARNED		
SPANISH NATIONAL RR CHAMPIONSHIPS	1	2008, 2015, 2019
GIRO DEL LAZIO/ROMA MAXIMA	1	2014

ADDITIONAL ALEJANDRO VALVERDE CONTINUED ON THE NEXT PAGE...

RACE	POINTS	YEARS
MINOR TOURS AND STAGE RACES – 18 POINTS EARNED		
VOLTA A CATALUNYA/TOUR OF CATALONIA	3	2009, 2017, 2018
TOUR OF THE BASQUE COUNTRY/VUELTA CICLISTA AL PAIS VASCO	3	2017
CRITÉRIUM DU DAUPHINÉ/CRITÉRIUM DU DAUPHINÉ LIBÉRÉ	3	2008, 2009
GRAND TOURS (VARIOUS POINTS) - 17 POINTS EARNED		
GIRO D'ITALIA		
3RD PLACE	1	2016
TOUR DE FRANCE		
3RD PLACE	2	2015
VUELTA A ESPAÑA (TOUR OF SPAIN)		
1ST PLACE	5	2009
2ND PLACE	2	2006, 2012, 2019
3RD PLACE	1	2003, 2013, 2014
GRAND TOUR CLASSIFICATION JERSEYS – 8 POINTS EARNED		
VUELTA A ESPAÑA: POINTS	2	2012, 2013, 2015, 2018

RACE	POINTS	YEARS
GRAND TOUR STAGE WINS - 10 POINTS EARNED		
GIRO D'ITALIA: 1 STAGE	½ POINT	2016
TOUR DE FRANCE: 4 STAGES	½ POINT	2005-2012
VUELTA A ESPAÑA: 13 STAGES, 2 TTT	½ POINT	2003-2019
SEASON-LONG COMPETITIONS – 10 POINTS EARNED		
UCI PROTOUR COMPETITION	2	2006, 2008
UCI WORLD TOUR	2	2014, 2015
UCI WORLD RANKING	2	2018
HOUR RECORD - 0 POINTS EARNED		
RACE RECORDS (VARIOUS POINTS) – 0 POINTS EARNED		
LIFETIME ACHIEVEMENTS (VARIOUS POINTS) – 10 POINTS EARNED		
ACHIEVED AT LEAST ONE VICTORY IN EVERY ROAD CATEGORY: 10 POINTS		

Rank 11: Miguel Induráin

BORN: **JULY 16, 1964**
YEARS ACTIVE: **1984-1996**
COUNTRY: **SPAIN**
NICKNAME: **BIG MIG,**
MIGUELÓN

CAREER WINS: **91**
TOTAL POINTS: **112**
RAW SCORE: **104**

AFTER ANQUETIL, "BIG MIG" IS THE NEXT GRAND TOUR SPECIALIST TO MAKE THE LIST. Induráin did win the 1990 Clásica de San Sebastián and the 1992 Spanish Road Race Championship, and was also on the podium three times in the World Road Race Championships, but the rest of his points were earned in either stage races or time trials. Also, like Anquetil, Induráin's success in Grand Tour victories—five Tours and two Giro—can be directly attributed to his phenomenal time trialing abilities. In fact, all but two of his sixteen Grand Tour stage wins were in a time trial or prologue. "Big Mig" also won the UCI Road World Ranking competition in 1992 and 1993, in large part due to the points earned in his back-to-back victories in the Giro and Tour in both of those years. It's no surprise that he broke the hour record in 1994, but like Moser and Tony Rominger after him, Induráin's performance was moved to the UCI Best Human Effort category, and no points were earned for the record.

RACE	POINTS	YEARS
THE MONUMENTS – 0 POINTS EARNED		
WORLD CHAMPIONSHIP ROAD RACE – 5 POINTS EARNED		
SILVER	2	1993, 1995
BRONZE	1	1991
CLASSICS/OLYMPICS/TIME TRIALS – 6 POINTS EARNED		
OLYMPIC TT GOLD	2	1996
WORLD TT GOLD	2	1995
CLÁSICA DE SAN SEBASTIÁN	2	1990
SEMI-CLASSICS/NATIONALS – 1 POINT EARNED		
NATIONAL CHAMPIONSHIPS	1	1992
MINOR TOURS AND STAGE RACES – 25 POINTS EARNED		
PARIS-NICE	3	1989, 1990
VOLTA A CATALUNYA/TOUR OF CATALONIA	3	1988, 1991, 1992
CRITÉRIUM DU DAUPHINÉ/CRITÉRIUM DU DAUPHINÉ LIBÉRÉ	3	1995, 1996
CRITÉRIUM INTERNATIONAL	2	1989
GP MIDI LIBRE	2	1995
GRAND TOURS (VARIOUS POINTS) – 55 POINTS EARNED		
GIRO D'ITALIA		
1ST PLACE	6	1992, 1993
3RD PLACE	1	1994
TOUR DE FRANCE		
1ST PLACE	8	1991, 1992, 1993, 1994, 1995
VUELTA A ESPAÑA (TOUR OF SPAIN)		
2ND PLACE	2	1991
GRAND TOUR CLASSIFICATION JERSEYS – 0 POINTS EARNED		

ADDITIONAL MIGUEL INDURÁIN CONTINUED ON THE NEXT PAGE...

RACE	POINTS	YEARS
GRAND TOUR STAGE WINS – 8 POINTS EARNED		
GIRO D'ITALIA: 4 STAGES	½ POINT	1992–1993
TOUR DE FRANCE: 12 STAGES	½ POINT	1989–1995
SEASON-LONG COMPETITIONS – 4 POINTS EARNED		
UCI ROAD WORLD ROAD RANKINGS	2	1992, 1993
HOUR RECORD – 0 POINTS EARNED		
RACE RECORDS (VARIOUS POINTS) – 8 POINTS EARNED		
TOUR DE FRANCE: 8 POINTS (SHARED WITH JACQUES ANQUETIL, EDDY MERCKX, AND BERNARD HINAULT)		
LIFETIME ACHIEVEMENTS (VARIOUS POINTS) – 0 POINTS EARNED		

Rank 12: Felice Gimondi

BORN: **SEPTEMBER 29, 1942**
YEARS ACTIVE: **1965-1979**
COUNTRY: **ITALY**
NICKNAME: **THE PHOENIX**

CAREER WINS: **78**
TOTAL POINTS: **112**
RAW SCORE: **92**

HE HAS THE FEWEST VICTORIES OF ANY IN THE TOP 12, but he definitely had a knack for winning prestigious races. He won the Worlds, Paris-Roubaix, Milan-San Remo, the Giro di Lombardia, and all three Grand Tours by 1968, the second to do so after Jacques Anquetil. Gimondi's huge breakthrough came in his first season as a professional in 1965. He wasn't even expecting to start the Tour de France that rookie year, but was a last-minute addition to the Salvarani squad when others became sick or injured. When his team's leader—Vittorio Adorni—and the current race leader, Bernard van de Kerckhove, had to abandon the race in the Pyrenees, Gimondi took possession of the yellow jersey after stage nine. The young Italian rode with a maturity well beyond his twenty-two years, and held the lead all the way to the finish, defeating none other than Raymond Poulidor. The following year, "The Phoenix" won Paris-Roubaix, Paris-Brussels, and the Giro di Lombardia. In 1967 he continued his progress up the ranks of cycling superstardom by winning that year's Giro against such luminaries as Franco Balmamion, Jacques Anquetil, Vittorio Adorni, Gianni Motta,

Lucien Aimar, and second-year pro, Eddy Merckx. Of course, the great Merckx matured the following year, and it would be another five years before Gimondi would again beat Merckx in a race. It's not that Gimondi didn't win big races, but time and again, he would find himself on the lower step of the podium in any head-to-head competition against "The Cannibal."

His luck finally changed in the 1973 World Championship Road Race in Barcelona when he found himself in a legendary four-man breakaway with Luis Ocaña, Merckx, and Freddy Maertens. Since both Merckx and Maertens were on the same team, the other two looked doomed to fight for a silver medal. Yet, somehow the Belgians managed to botch their signals, and Gimondi outsprinted them all to become the gold medalist. The five-year monkey was finally off of his back. He went on to win the 1974 Milan-San Remo and, at the age of thirty-three, captured the 1976 Giro d'Italia. Oddly, Merckx would finish down in eighth place in that race, only one spot ahead of where he'd finished to Gimondi the last time he was defeated by the Italian in a Grand Tour, nine years earlier in 1967. Gimondi retired in 1978 and became one of the most revered cyclists of his generation. Sadly, we lost one of our cherished cycling icons in the summer of 2019 when he suffered a heart attack while swimming off the coast in Sicily.

RACE	POINTS	YEARS
THE MONUMENTS – 13 POINTS EARNED		
MILAN–SAN REMO:	3	1974
PARIS-ROUBAIX	4	1966
IL LOMBARDIA/GIRO DI LOMBARDIA	3	1966, 1973

ADDITIONAL FELICE GIMONDI CONTINUED ON THE NEXT PAGE...

RACE	POINTS	YEARS
WORLD CHAMPIONSHIP ROAD RACE - 7 POINTS EARNED		
GOLD	4	1973
SILVER	2	1971
BRONZE	1	1970
CLASSICS/OLYMPICS/TIME TRIALS – 6 POINTS EARNED		
PARIS–BRUSSELS	2	1966
GRAND PRIX DE NATIONS	2	1967, 1968
SEMI-CLASSICS/NATIONALS – 10 POINTS EARNED		
ITALIAN NATIONAL RR CHAMPIONSHIPS	1	1968, 1972
GIRO DEL LAZIO	1	1967
BRUSSELS CYCLING CLASSIC/PARIS-BRUSSELS	1	1976
GIRO DELLA ROMAGNA		SERVED AS THE 1968 NATIONAL RR CHAMPIONSHIP
GRAN PIEMONTE/GIRO DEL PIEMONTE	1	1971, 1973
COPPA PLACCI	1	1966
CRITÉRIUM DES AS	1	1968
TROFEO BARACCHI	1	1968 (WITH JACQUES ANQUETIL), 1973 (WITH MARTIN EMILIO RODRIGUEZ)
MINOR TOURS AND STAGE RACES – 6 POINTS EARNED		
VOLTA A CATALUNYA/TOUR OF CATALONIA	3	1972
TOUR OF ROMANDY	3	1969

RACE	POINTS	YEARS
GRAND TOURS (VARIOUS POINTS) - 43 POINTS EARNED		
GIRO D'ITALIA		
1ST PLACE	6	1967, 1969, 1976
2ND PLACE	3	1970, 1973
3RD PLACE	1	1965, 1968, 1974
TOUR DE FRANCE		
1ST PLACE	8	1965
2ND PLACE	4	1972
VUELTA A ESPAÑA (TOUR OF SPAIN)		
1ST PLACE (PRE 1974)	4	1968
GRAND TOUR CLASSIFICATION JERSEYS – 0 POINTS EARNED		
GRAND TOUR STAGE WINS - 7 POINTS EARNED		
GIRO D'ITALIA: 6 STAGES	½ POINT	1966–1976
TOUR DE FRANCE: 7 STAGES	½ POINT	1965–1975
VUELTA A ESPAÑA: 1 STAGE	½ POINT	1968
SEASON-LONG COMPETITIONS – 0 POINTS EARNED		
HOUR RECORD - 0 POINTS EARNED		
RACE RECORDS (VARIOUS POINTS) – 0 POINTS EARNED		
LIFETIME ACHIEVEMENTS (VARIOUS POINTS) – 20 POINTS EARNED		
WON ALL THREE GRAND TOURS: 10 POINTS		
WON 3 OF ANY 5 MONUMENTS AND ANY GRAND TOUR: 10 POINTS		

Rank 13: Louison Bobet

BORN: **MARCH 12, 1925**
YEARS ACTIVE: **1947-1961**
COUNTRY: **FRANCE**
NICKNAME:
THE BAKER OF SAINT-MÉEN

CAREER WINS: **63**
TOTAL POINTS: **103.5**
RAW SCORE: **83.5**

BOBET TURNED PROFESSIONAL IN 1946 and didn't win his first Tour
de France until 1953. It was a long eight-year wait, but he then went
on a roll and became the first three-time winner, and in consecutive
years for good measure. He is only one of seven cyclists to win a
race in every major category (along with Merckx, Hinault, Kübler,
Janssen, Moser, and Valverde). Bobet also captured every Monument
save Liège, which is odd since it's the one single-day race victory
you'd expect to see on his *palmarès*.

After Bobet conquered the Tour three times in a row, it was
time to set his sights on new goals. He skipped the Grand Tours
altogether in 1956, instead focusing on the spring classics—the
fruits of those efforts a win in Paris-Roubaix against a legendary
field of competitors that included both Rik Van Looy and Rik Van
Steenbergen. In 1957 he opted to forego the Tour once again, with
the plan of becoming the first Frenchman to win the Giro d'Italia.

That objective would most likely have been met, had it not been for Charly Gaul, who detested Bobet's somewhat pretentious, movie star personality. During the second to last mountain stage, Gaul lead the race by fifty-six seconds and was well positioned to repeat his 1956 victory. As the group containing Bobet passed Gaul while he was relieving himself at the side of the road, the Luxembourger inexplicably turned around and starting making obscene gestures with the object of his manhood. Infuriated, Bobet organized and launched a vicious attack, the French and Italian teams working together to distance themselves from the race leader. By the end of the stage, Gaul had lost all hope of winning the Giro, finishing over eight-and-a-half minutes back of Bobet's group; his infantile behavior had cost him a Grand Tour victory. At the start of the next stage, Bobet was only trailing the lead of Italian Gastone Nencini by a mere nineteen seconds, and he launched an attack along with his teammate Rafaël Géminiani on the final climb of the race, the Brocon. He was well on his way to taking the lead; Nencini had flatted while descending the previous climb and had lost contact with the lead group. The Italian's race looked to be lost, but Gaul chose to use Nencini's misfortune to exact his revenge on his hated rival. Gaul waited for Nencini and then proceeded to bury himself by pacing Nencini back to Bobet's small lead group, catching them and even winning the stage. "The Angel of the Mountains" had towed the race leader back to Bobet's wheel, and the Frenchman's Giro was lost—only two flat stages remained and there was simply nowhere left to make up the needed time. Nencini won the 1957 Giro with a slim nineteen-second margin, to this day one of closest finishes in its history. That race became known as the *Giro di cheri–pipi*—"Giro of the dearest piss" (although I have also seen it translated as "Giro of the costly piss"). I'm sure that neither Gaul nor Bobet were amused by the charming *sobriquet*.

ADDITIONAL LOUISON BOBET CONTINUED ON THE NEXT PAGE...

"The Baker of St. Méen" ended up with *palmarès* that included wins in four of the five Monuments, a World Championship, five Minor Tours, three Grand Tours, thirteen GT stages, two mountains classifications, and the Challenge Desgrange-Columbo (the official season-long competition). Bobet accumulated this phenomenal list of victories despite being plagued by saddle sores throughout his career. It's even suspected that the horrible boils he suffered in the 1955 Tour de France were actually caused by cancer, an illness to which he finally succumbed at the age of fifty-eight.

RACE	POINTS	YEARS
THE MONUMENTS – 13 POINTS EARNED		
MILAN–SAN REMO:	3	1951
TOUR OF FLANDERS/RONDE VAN VLAANDEREN	3	1955
PARIS-ROUBAIX	4	1956
IL LOMBARDIA/GIRO DI LOMBARDIA	3	1951
WORLD CHAMPIONSHIP ROAD RACE - 7 POINTS EARNED		
GOLD	4	1954
SILVER	2	1957
BRONZE	1	1958
CLASSICS/OLYMPICS/TIME TRIALS – 6 POINTS EARNED		
BORDEAUX–PARIS	2	1959
GRAND PRIX DE NATIONS	2	1952, 1953
SEMI-CLASSICS/NATIONALS – 8 POINTS EARNED		
FRENCH NATIONAL RR CHAMPIONSHIPS	1	1950, 1951
CRITÉRIUM NATIONAL DE LA ROUTE	1	1951, 1952
CRITÉRIUM DES AS	1	1949, 1950, 1953, 1954

RACE	POINTS	YEARS
MINOR TOURS AND STAGE RACES – 8 POINTS EARNED		
PARIS-NICE	3	1952
CRITÉRIUM DU DAUPHINÉ/CRITÉRIUM DU DAUPHINÉ LIBÉRÉ	3	1955
TOUR DE LUXEMBOURG	2	1955
GRAND TOURS (VARIOUS POINTS) - 29 POINTS EARNED		
GIRO D'ITALIA		
2ND PLACE	3	1957
TOUR DE FRANCE		
1ST PLACE	8	1953, 1954, 1955
3RD PLACE	2	1950
GRAND TOUR CLASSIFICATION JERSEYS – 4 POINTS EARNED		
GIRO D'ITALIA: MOUNTAINS	2	1951
TOUR DE FRANCE: MOUNTAINS	2	1950
GRAND TOUR STAGE WINS – 6.5 POINTS EARNED		
GIRO D'ITALIA: 2 STAGES	½ POINT	1951-1957
TOUR DE FRANCE: 11 STAGES	½ POINT	1948-1955
SEASON-LONG COMPETITIONS – 2 POINTS EARNED		
DESGRANGE–COLOMBO TROPHY	2	1951
HOUR RECORD - 0 POINTS EARNED		
RACE RECORDS (VARIOUS POINTS) – 0 POINTS EARNED		
LIFETIME ACHIEVEMENTS (VARIOUS POINTS) – 20 POINTS EARNED		
ACHIEVED AT LEAST ONE VICTORY IN EVERY ROAD CATEGORY: 10 POINTS		
WON 3 OF ANY 5 MONUMENTS AND ANY GRAND TOUR: 10 POINTS		

Rank 14: Laurent Jalabert

BORN: **NOVEMBER 30, 1968**
YEARS ACTIVE: **1989-2002**
COUNTRY: **FRANCE**
NICKNAME:
JAJA / LE PANDA (THE PANDA)

CAREER WINS: **141**
TOTAL POINTS: **99.5**
RAW SCORE: **89.5**

JALABERT STARTED OUT HIS CAREER AS A SPRINTER, but a horrible crash in the dash for the finish line in the first stage of the 1994 Tour de France convinced him to pursue different goals. He became a true all-rounder and went on to win a race in every category, except the World Championship RR, in which he did get close by placing second in 1992. As a testament to his versatility, not only did he win the 1995 Tour of Spain, but also both the points and mountains classifications in that same race. It is only Eddy Merckx and Tony Rominger who have also managed this rare feat of securing all three jerseys in one Grand Tour.

In total, "JaJa" claimed nine classification competitions—seven points classifications earned in all three GTs, and one mountains classification in both the Tour and Vuelta—earning him an extra ten points in Career Milestone Adjustments. Jalabert was a prolific Minor Tour and stage race winner, capturing 10 victories over his career. He also won Milan-San Remo in 1995, the Giro di Lombardia in 1997, La Flèche Wallonne in 1995 and 1997, the Clásica de San Sebastián in 2001, and was French National RR Champion in 1998. Jalabert captured twenty-five Grand Tour stages, three in Italy, four in France, and eighteen in Spain. As further evidence of his well-rounded abilities, Jalabert also captured four straight season-long competitions from 1995 to 1999 (at the time the UCI World Ranking). Like Alejandro Valverde, you have to wonder if he might have won a few more Grand Tours had he not struggled with high altitude.

RACE	POINTS	YEARS
THE MONUMENTS – 6 POINTS EARNED		
MILAN–SAN REMO:	3	1995
IL LOMBARDIA/GIRO DI LOMBARDIA	3	1997
WORLD CHAMPIONSHIP ROAD RACE – 2 POINTS EARNED		
SILVER	2	1992
CLASSICS/OLYMPICS/TIME TRIALS – 10 POINTS EARNED		
WORLD TT GOLD	2	1997
LA FLÈCHE WALLONNE	2	1995, 1997
CLÁSICA DE SAN SEBASTIÁN	2	2001, 2002
SEMI-CLASSICS/NATIONALS – 2 POINTS EARNED		
FRENCH NATIONAL RR CHAMPIONSHIPS	1	1998
MILANO–TORINO/MILAN–TURIN	1	1997
MINOR TOURS AND STAGE RACES – 26 POINTS EARNED		
PARIS-NICE	3	1995, 1996, 1997
VOLTA A CATALUNYA/TOUR OF CATALONIA	3	1995
TOUR OF THE BASQUE COUNTRY/VUELTA CICLISTA AL PAIS VASCO	3	1999
TOUR OF ROMANDY	3	1999
CRITÉRIUM INTERNATIONAL	2	1995
CATALAN WEEK/SETMANA CATALUNYA	2	1999, 2000
GP MIDI LIBRE	2	1996

ADDITIONAL LAURENT JALABERT CONTINUED ON THE NEXT PAGE...

RACE	POINTS	YEARS
GRAND TOURS (VARIOUS POINTS) - 5 POINTS EARNED		
VUELTA A ESPAÑA (TOUR OF SPAIN)		
1ST PLACE	5	1995
GRAND TOUR CLASSIFICATION JERSEYS – 18 POINTS EARNED		
GIRO D'ITALIA: POINTS	2	1999
TOUR DE FRANCE: POINTS	2	1992, 1995
VUELTA A ESPAÑA: POINTS	2	1994, 1995, 1996, 1997
TOUR DE FRANCE: MOUNTAINS	2	2001
VUELTA A ESPAÑA: MOUNTAINS	2	1995
GRAND TOUR STAGE WINS - 12.5 POINTS EARNED		
GIRO D'ITALIA: 3 STAGES	½ POINT	1999
TOUR DE FRANCE: 4 STAGES	½ POINT	1992-2001
VUELTA A ESPAÑA: 18 STAGES	½ POINT	1993-1997
SEASON-LONG COMPETITIONS – 8 POINTS EARNED		
UCI ROAD WORLD ROAD RANKINGS	2	1995, 1996, 1997, 1999
HOUR RECORD - 0 POINTS EARNED		
RACE RECORDS (VARIOUS POINTS) – 0 POINTS EARNED		
LIFETIME ACHIEVEMENTS (VARIOUS POINTS) – 10 POINTS EARNED		
WON ANY EIGHT GRAND TOUR CLASSIFICATION JERSEYS: 10 POINTS		

Rank 15: Freddy Maertens

BORN: **FEBRUARY, 13, 1952**
YEARS ACTIVE: **1972-1985**
COUNTRY: **BELGIUM**
NICKNAME: **THE OGRE**

CAREER WINS: **148**
TOTAL POINTS: **99**
RAW SCORE: **89**

I'VE RECALCULATED MAERTEN'S TOTALS MANY TIMES, thinking I must have somehow made a mistake. It's hard to believe that somebody won so many races in such a short period of time. Next to Merckx, he has the single-highest point totals earned in a single season, thirty, which he earned in the 1977 season. From 1976–1978 he won the World Championship Road Race, two season-long competitions, a staggering thirty-one Grand Tour stages, four Classics, eight Semi-Classics, six Minor Tours, four Grand Tour points classifications, and the 1977 Vuelta, also claiming thirteen of its stages, which is a GT record that still stands. Despite that incredible victory count, Maertens didn't win a single Monument over that stretch, or for that matter, over the course of his entire career.

Oddly, Maertens didn't score a single point in 1979 or 1980, and then rose from the dead in 1981 to win an incredible five stages in that year's Tour de France (along with another points classification), followed up by yet another World Championship RR title. That gold medal in the 1981 event was the last race he would win before retiring in 1986. Strange indeed, but alcoholism and financial troubles, which included tax evasion, were said to have played a large part in his erratic performances. Given his incredible output over a three-year span, you have to wonder if he'd have ended up a lot higher on this list without all the drama in his personal life. I'm sure he'd have added a Monument or two to his already impressive *palmarès*.

RACE	POINTS	YEARS
THE MONUMENTS – 0 POINTS EARNED		
WORLD CHAMPIONSHIP ROAD RACE – 10 POINTS EARNED		
GOLD	4	1976, 1981
SILVER	2	1973
CLASSICS/OLYMPICS/TIME TRIALS – 12 POINTS EARNED		
GHENT–WEVELGEM	2	1975, 1976
AMSTEL GOLD	2	1976
PARIS–TOURS	2	1975
CHAMPIONSHIP OF ZURICH/ZURI–METZGETE	2	1976
GRAND PRIX DE NATIONS	2	1976

ADDITIONAL FREDDY MAERTENS CONTINUED ON THE NEXT PAGE...

RACE	POINTS	YEARS
SEMI-CLASSICS/NATIONALS – 10 POINTS EARNED		
BELGIAN NATIONAL RR CHAMPIONSHIPS	1	1976
OMLOOP HET NIEUWSBLAD/HET VOLK	1	1977, 1978
E3 BINKBANK CLASSIC/E3 HARELBEKE/HARELBEKE–ANTWERP–HARELBEKE/E3 PRIJS VLAANDEREN	1	1978
BRABANTSE PIJL/FLÈCHE BRABANÇONNE	1	1976
SCHELDEPRIJS/GP DE L'ESCAUT/GROTE SCHELDEPRIJS/ SCHELDEPRIJS VLAANDEREN	1	1973
ESCHBORN-FRANKFURT/FRANKFURT GRAND PRIX/ RUND UM DEN HENNINGER-TURN	1	1976
BRUSSELS CYCLING CLASSIC/PARIS-BRUSSELS (POST 1966 EDITIONS)	1	1975
CRITÉRIUM DES AS	1	1976
TROFEO BARACCHI	1	1976 (WITH MICHEL POLLENTIER)
MINOR TOURS AND STAGE RACES – 22 POINTS EARNED		
PARIS-NICE	3	1977
VOLTA A CATALUNYA/TOUR OF CATALONIA	3	1977
CATALAN WEEK/SETMANA CATALUNYA	2	1977
GIRO DI SARDEGNA	2	1977
FOUR DAYS OF DUNKIRK	2	1973, 1975, 1976, 1978
TOUR OF BELGIUM	2	1975
TOUR DE LUXEMBOURG	2	1974

RACE	POINTS	YEARS
GRAND TOURS (VARIOUS POINTS) - 5 POINTS EARNED		
VUELTA A ESPAÑA (TOUR OF SPAIN)		
IST PLACE (1974-PRESENT)	5	1977
GRAND TOUR CLASSIFICATION JERSEYS – 8 POINTS EARNED		
TOUR DE FRANCE: POINTS	2	1976, 1978, 1981
VUELTA A ESPAÑA: POINTS	2	1977
GRAND TOUR STAGE WINS - 18 POINTS EARNED		
GIRO D'ITALIA: 7 STAGES	½ POINT	1977
TOUR DE FRANCE: 16 STAGES	½ POINT	1976-1981
VUELTA A ESPAÑA: 13 STAGES	½ POINT	1977
SEASON-LONG COMPETITIONS – 4 POINTS EARNED		
SUPER PRESTIGE PERNOD TROPHY	2	1976, 1977
HOUR RECORD - 0 POINTS EARNED		
RACE RECORDS (VARIOUS POINTS) – 0 POINTS EARNED		
LIFETIME ACHIEVEMENTS (VARIOUS POINTS) – 10 POINTS EARNED		
WON 30 GRAND TOUR STAGES: 10 PTS		

Rank 16: Chris Froome

BORN: **MAY 20, 1985**
YEARS ACTIVE: **2007–PRESENT**
COUNTRY: **GREAT BRITAIN**
NICKNAME: **FROOMEY**

CAREER WINS: **47**
TOTAL POINTS: **98.5**
RAW SCORE: **88.5**

AT THE START OF THE 2019 SEASON, it was hard to imagine that "Froomey" wouldn't be moving higher up on this list, but then disaster struck during a recon of June's Dauphiné time trial stage – a horrible crash left him with a compound fracture to his femur, along with fractures to his hip, elbow, and neck. After the 2018 season, Froome had secured twelve Grand Tour podiums, seven of those outright victories, which also included a win in the 2011 Vuelta which was awarded to him in July of 2019 when Juan Jose Cobo failed to appeal the decision of the UCI to enforce a retroactive doping ban. Froome will turn thirty-five in May 2020, so if he can recover from his injuries and return to the top level of the sport, he will probably have another two or three seasons to add to his Grand Tour tally. Should he bank a single victory in any one of those races before the end of his career, he'll join the exclusive club of Merckx, Anquetil, and Hinault as the only other cyclists to have won eight Grand Tours; he'd receive a huge fifteen-point bonus for that achievement and crack the Top 10.

RACE	POINTS	YEARS
THE MONUMENTS – 0 POINTS EARNED		
WORLD CHAMPIONSHIP ROAD RACE – 0 POINTS EARNED		
CLASSICS/OLYMPICS/TIME TRIALS – 0 POINTS EARNED		
SEMI-CLASSICS/NATIONALS – 0 POINTS EARNED		
MINOR TOURS AND STAGE RACES – 17 POINTS EARNED		
TOUR OF ROMANDY	3	2013, 2014
CRITÉRIUM DU DAUPHINÉ/CRITÉRIUM DU DAUPHINÉ LIBÉRÉ	3	2013, 2015, 2016
CRITÉRIUM INTERNATIONAL	2	2013
GRAND TOURS (VARIOUS POINTS) – 58 POINTS EARNED		
GIRO D'ITALIA		
1ST PLACE	6	2018
TOUR DE FRANCE		
1ST PLACE	8	2013, 2015, 2016, 2017
2ND PLACE	4	2012
3RD PLACE	2	2018
VUELTA A ESPAÑA (TOUR OF SPAIN)		
1ST PLACE (1974-PRESENT)	5	2011, 2017
2ND PLACE	2	2014, 2016

ADDITIONAL CHRIS FROOME CONTINUED ON THE NEXT PAGE...

RACE	POINTS	YEARS
GRAND TOUR CLASSIFICATION JERSEYS – 6 POINTS EARNED		
VUELTA A ESPAÑA: POINTS	2	2017
GIRO D'ITALIA: MOUNTAINS	2	2018
TOUR DE FRANCE: MOUNTAINS	2	2015
GRAND TOUR STAGE WINS – 7.5 POINTS EARNED		
GIRO D'ITALIA: 2 STAGES	½ POINT	2018
TOUR DE FRANCE: 7 STAGES	½ POINT	2013-2017
VUELTA A ESPAÑA: 5 STAGES, 1 TTT	½ POINT	2011-2017
SEASON-LONG COMPETITIONS – 0 POINTS EARNED		
HOUR RECORD – 0 POINTS EARNED		
RACE RECORDS (VARIOUS POINTS) – 0 POINTS EARNED		
LIFETIME ACHIEVEMENTS (VARIOUS POINTS) – 10 POINTS EARNED		
WON ALL THREE GRAND TOURS: 10 POINTS		

Rank 17: Ferdi Kübler

BORN: **JULY 24, 1919**
YEARS ACTIVE: **1940-1957**
COUNTRY: **SWITZERLAND**
NICKNAME: **THE COWBOY /
MR. 100,000 VOLTS**

CAREER WINS: **71**
TOTAL POINTS: **94.5**
RAW SCORE: **68.5**

HE'S ANOTHER ONE OF THOSE RARE CYCLISTS who seemed to have
a knack for winning the most important races on the calendar, and
in recognition of this feat, he received bonus points for winning a
race in every category. What makes this milestone unique is that
like both Coppi and Bartali, he lost a chunk of his career to World
War II (he turned pro in 1940), yet neither of those two legends
were able to match that particular accomplishment. An even rarer
feat was Kübler's La Flèche Wallone and Liège-Bastogne-Liège wins
in the same year, this back in the days when the races were held on
the same weekend. He did this not just once but unbelievably twice
in back-to-back years (1951 and 1952), a testament to his regular
regimen of training rides lasting six to eight hours.

His win in the 1951 Flèche was legendary. Kübler outsprinted
his breakaway companions, who included Gino Bartali, Louison
Bobet, and Jean Robic. This small group was in turn being chased
by another that included such luminaries as Fiorenzo Magni, Rik
Van Steenbergen, Raymond Impanis, and Marcel Kint; it was truly
cycling's Golden Age in full bloom. It's no wonder that one of

Kübler's nicknames was "Mr. 100,000 Volts." Of course, nowadays he'd be called "Mr. 100,000 Watts." That prodigious power was used to amass a *palmarès* that included three Liège-Bastogne-Liège, a gold in the World Championship RR, four Classics, five National RR titles, five Minor Tours, the 1950 Tour de France, the 1954 Tour points classification, eight stages in the Tour, and three season-long competitions; he was one of the great all-rounders in the history of the sport.

RACE	POINTS	YEARS
THE MONUMENTS - 6 POINTS EARNED		
LIÈGE-BASTOGNE-LIÈGE	3	1951, 1952
WORLD CHAMPIONSHIP ROAD RACE - 7 POINTS EARNED		
GOLD	4	1951
SILVER	2	1949
BRONZE	1	1950
CLASSICS/OLYMPICS/TIME TRIALS - 8 POINTS EARNED		
LA FLÈCHE WALLONNE	2	1951, 1952
CHAMPIONSHIP OF ZURICH/ZÜRI-METZGETE	2	1943
BORDEAUX-PARIS	2	1953
SEMI-CLASSICS/NATIONALS - 6 POINTS EARNED		
SWISS NATIONAL RR CHAMPIONSHIPS	1	1948, 1949, 1950, 1951, 1954
MILANO-TORINO/MILAN-TURIN	1	1956
MINOR TOURS AND STAGE RACES - 15 POINTS EARNED		
TOUR OF ROMANDY	3	1942, 1948, 1951
TOUR OF SWITZERLAND/TOUR DE SUISSE	3	1948, 1951

ADDITIONAL FERDI KÜBLER CONTINUED ON THE NEXT PAGE...

RACE	POINTS	YEARS
GRAND TOURS (VARIOUS POINTS) - 14 POINTS EARNED		
GIRO D'ITALIA		
3RD PLACE	1	1951, 1952
TOUR DE FRANCE		
IST PLACE	8	1950
2ND PLACE	4	1954
GRAND TOUR CLASSIFICATION JERSEYS - 2 POINTS EARNED		
TOUR DE FRANCE: POINTS	2	1954
GRAND TOUR STAGE WINS - 4.5 POINTS EARNED		
TOUR DE FRANCE: 8 STAGES, I TTT	½ POINT	1947-1954
SEASON-LONG COMPETITIONS - 6 POINTS EARNED		
DESGRANGE–COLOMBO TROPHY	2	1950, 1952, 1954
HOUR RECORD - 0 POINTS EARNED		
RACE RECORDS (VARIOUS POINTS) - 0 POINTS EARNED		
LIFETIME ACHIEVEMENTS (VARIOUS POINTS) - 26 POINTS EARNED		
ACHIEVED AT LEAST ONE VICTORY IN EVERY ROAD CATEGORY: 10 POINTS		
MISSING YEARS ADJUSTMENT: 16 POINTS		

Rank 18: Tony Rominger

BORN: **MARCH 27, 1961**
YEARS ACTIVE: **1986–1997**
COUNTRY: **SWITZERLAND**
NICKNAME: **THE HAMMER**

CAREER WINS: **94**
TOTAL POINTS: **90.5**
RAW SCORE: **90.5**

BACK WHEN INDURÁIN WAS ON HIS Tour de France rampage, I remember Rominger was always touted as a possible contender for the race, but always fell out of contention due to his problems with hayfever. Over the course of his eleven-year career, the only points Rominger earned in summer races were the four points he earned by finishing second in the 1993 Tour, along with the two points for capturing the mountains classification in that same race; outside of that, nothing.

Nearly a third of Rominger's points were earned in the early-season, weeklong stage races, which included two Paris-Nice, two Tirreno-Adriatico, three Tour of the Basque Country, two Tour of Romandy, and one Setmana Catalana. It's interesting to note that all three of his Vuelta wins occurred when the race was still held in April, right before the race was moved to its current calendar position in August/September. Along with Merckx and Jalabert, Rominger is the only cyclist to have captured all three jerseys in a single Grand

Tour—first place, points, and mountains, which he accomplished in the 1993 Vuelta. His late-season successes included two wins in the Giro di Lombardia and two Grand Prix de Nations. Since he fared so poorly in the heat, it's surprising that he didn't try to win the Giro more often. He only entered the race once in the last eight years of his career, in 1995. Not only did he win that year, but he lead the race from the second stage on, claimed four stages, and also captured the points classification. Rominger also set the hour record, but like Moser and Induráin, had his benchmark moved to the UCI Best Human Effort category in 1997, and as a result earned no points for the accomplishment.

RACE	POINTS	YEARS
THE MONUMENTS - 6 POINTS EARNED		
IL LOMBARDIA/GIRO DI LOMBARDIA	3	1989, 1992
WORLD CHAMPIONSHIP ROAD RACE - 0 POINTS EARNED		
CLASSICS/OLYMPICS/TIME TRIALS - 4 POINTS EARNED		
GRAND PRIX DE NATIONS	2	1991, 1994
SEMI-CLASSICS/NATIONALS - 1 POINT EARNED		
GIRO DELL'EMILIA	1	1988
MINOR TOURS AND STAGE RACES - 31 POINTS EARNED		
PARIS-NICE	3	1991, 1994
TIRRENO-ADRIATICO	3	1989, 1990
TOUR OF THE BASQUE COUNTRY/VUELTA CICLISTA AL PAIS VASCO	3	1992, 1993, 1994
TOUR OF ROMANDY	3	1991, 1995
CATALAN WEEK/SETMANA CATALUNYA	2	1993

ADDITIONAL TONY ROMINGER CONTINUED ON THE NEXT PAGE...

RACE	POINTS	YEARS
GRAND TOURS (VARIOUS POINTS) - 26 POINTS EARNED		
GIRO D'ITALIA		
1ST PLACE	6	1995
TOUR DE FRANCE		
2ND PLACE	4	1993
VUELTA A ESPAÑA (TOUR OF SPAIN)		
1ST PLACE (1974-PRESENT)	5	1992, 1993, 1994
3RD PLACE	1	1996
GRAND TOUR CLASSIFICATION JERSEYS - 10 POINTS EARNED		
GIRO D'ITALIA: POINTS	2	1995
VUELTA A ESPAÑA: POINTS	2	1993
TOUR DE FRANCE: MOUNTAINS	2	1993
VUELTA A ESPAÑA: MOUNTAINS	2	1993, 1996
GRAND TOUR STAGE WINS - 10.5 POINTS EARNED		
GIRO D'ITALIA: 5 STAGES	½ POINT	1988-1995
TOUR DE FRANCE: 3 STAGES	½ POINT	1993
VUELTA A ESPAÑA: 13 STAGES	½ POINT	1992-1996
SEASON-LONG COMPETITIONS - 2 POINTS EARNED		
UCI ROAD WORLD ROAD RANKINGS	2	1994
HOUR RECORD - 0 POINTS EARNED		
RACE RECORDS (VARIOUS POINTS) - 0 POINTS EARNED		
LIFETIME ACHIEVEMENTS (VARIOUS POINTS) - 0 POINTS EARNED		

Rank 19: Fiorenzo Magni

BORN: **DECEMBER 7, 1920**
YEARS ACTIVE: **1940-1956**
COUNTRY: **ITALY**
NICKNAME:
**THE LION OF FLANDERS /
THE COLOSSUS OF MONZA**

CAREER WINS: **56**
TOTAL POINTS: **87.5**
RAW SCORE: **63.5**

MAGNI EXCELLED IN TOUGH RIDING CONDITIONS. When rain, wind, cold, and snow would crush others' souls, Magni would flourish. He won three straight editions of Flanders in 1949, 1950, and 1951 in atrocious weather, thus earning "The Lion of Flanders" nickname; he is the only cyclist to have won three consecutive editions of that race. This feat was also accomplished at a time when only one non-Belgian had ever won the race before. As further testament of his ability to excel in tough conditions, he placed second in the 1956 Giro after breaking not one, but two bones in two separate crashes. The first crash occurred during stage twelve, when he suffered a broken clavicle. The second crash occurred on a descent during stage sixteen, in which he broke his humerus and passed out from the horrible pain. Charly Gaul went on to win the race with a legendary attack during the freezing stage eighteen snow storm, but unbelievably, Magni also completed that stage, only one of forty-three riders to do so. He ended up finishing that Giro in second place, only 3 minutes, 27 seconds down. Had he not suffered through such terrible misfortune in that race, there's little doubt he would have added yet another victory in Italy's Grand Tour to those he'd already secured in 1948, 1951, and 1955.

He was considered Italy's "third man," since Magni competed at the same time as both Coppi and Bartali. Although the moniker was certainly true, it does little justice in painting an accurate picture of his significance to the cycling world. In 1952 he became the first cyclist to convince a company from outside the cycling industry to become a team backer. At a time when many bike manufacturers were failing and unable to provide the money required for team sponsorship, the Nivea skin cream company stepped up to the plate and forever changed the financial landscape of professional cycling. The sport's current success, in large part due to the backing of its many corporate sponsors, can be directly attributed to the efforts made by "The Colossus of Monza" back in 1952.

In addition to his three Giro victories and his Flanders three-peat, Magni also won twelve Italian Semi-Classics, three National RR Championships, three Trofeo Baracchi (a prestigious late-season, two-man invitational time trial), the 1955 Vuelta points classification, seven Tour de France stages, six Giro stages, and three Vuelta stages. He was quite the "third man."

RACE	POINTS	YEARS
THE MONUMENTS – 9 POINTS EARNED		
TOUR OF FLANDERS/RONDE VAN VLAANDEREN	3	1949, 1950, 1951
WORLD CHAMPIONSHIP ROAD RACE – 2 POINTS EARNED		
SILVER	2	1951
CLASSICS/OLYMPICS/TIME TRIALS – 0 POINTS EARNED		

ADDITIONAL FIORENZO MAGNI CONTINUED ON THE NEXT PAGE...

RACE	POINTS	YEARS
SEMI-CLASSICS/NATIONALS – 18 POINTS EARNED		
ITALIAN NATIONAL RR CHAMPIONSHIPS	1	1951, 1953, 1954
GIRO DEL LAZIO	1	1951, 1956
GIRO DELLA ROMAGNA	1	1951, 1955
GIRO DELLA TOSCANA	1	1949, 1954
MILANO–TORINO/MILAN–TURIN	1	1951
TRE VALLE VARESINE	1	1947
GRAN PIEMONTE/GIRO DEL PIEMONTE	1	1942, 1953, 1956
GIRO DEL VENETO	1	1953
TROFEO BARACCHI	1	1949 (WITH ADOLFO GROSSO), 1950 (WITH ANTONIO BEVILACQUA), 1951 (WITH GIUSEPPE MINARDI)
MINOR TOURS AND STAGE RACES – 0 POINTS EARNED		
GRAND TOURS (VARIOUS POINTS) - 24 POINTS EARNED		
GIRO D'ITALIA		
1ST PLACE	6	1948, 1951, 1955
2ND PLACE	3	1952, 1956
GRAND TOUR CLASSIFICATION JERSEYS – 2 POINTS EARNED		
VUELTA A ESPAÑA: POINTS	2	1955
GRAND TOUR STAGE WINS - 8 POINTS EARNED		
GIRO D'ITALIA: 6 STAGES	½ POINT	1948-1955
TOUR DE FRANCE: 7 STAGES	½ POINT	1949-1953
VUELTA A ESPAÑA: 3 STAGES, 1 TTT	½ POINT	1955

SEASON-LONG COMPETITIONS – 0 POINTS EARNED

HOUR RECORD - 0 POINTS EARNED

RACE RECORDS (VARIOUS POINTS) – 3 POINTS EARNED

TOUR OF FLANDERS: 3 POINTS (SHARED WITH ACHIEL BUYSSE, ERIC LEMAN, JOHAN MUSEEUW, TOM BOONEN, AND FABIAN CANCELLARA)

LIFETIME ACHIEVEMENTS (VARIOUS POINTS) – 21 POINTS EARNED

MISSING YEARS ADJUSTMENT: 21 POINTS

Rank 20: Giuseppe Saronni

BORN: **SEPTEMBER 22, 1957**
YEARS ACTIVE: **1977–1990**
COUNTRY: **ITALY**
NICKNAME: *BEPPE*

CAREER WINS: **145**
TOTAL POINTS: **86.5**
RAW SCORE: **86.5**

SARONNI WAS AN EXTREMELY WELL-ROUNDED CYCLIST and scored points in every category except one—he never captured a season-long competition. He was a prolific winner, but during the peak of his career, the Super Prestige Pernod Trophy was also up for grabs by the likes of Francesco Moser, Bernard Hinault, and Sean Kelly, so it's no surprise that Saronni finished second in the competition twice, and third once. Had he won even one of those trophies, he'd have picked up an extra ten points and moved another five places higher in the rankings.

In spite of that missing accomplishment, you don't make it to number twenty on this list without some significant wins—these included the 1983 Milan-San Remo, the 1982 Giro di Lombardia, the 1979 Zuri-Metzgete, the 1980 La Flèche Wallone, gold in the 1982 World Championship RR, eleven Semi-Classics, eight Minor Tours, two Giro d'Italia (1979 and 1983), four Giro points classifications, and twenty-seven Grand Tour stages. Given that Saronni and Moser competed at the same time, and vied for many of the same victories, it's easy to draw comparisons to Italy's other great rivalry between Coppi and Bartali, which had played out three decades earlier.

RACE	POINTS	YEARS
THE MONUMENTS – 6 POINTS EARNED		
MILAN–SAN REMO:	3	1983
IL LOMBARDIA/GIRO DI LOMBARDIA	3	1982
WORLD CHAMPIONSHIP ROAD RACE – 7 POINTS EARNED		
GOLD	4	1982
SILVER	2	1981
BRONZE	1	1986
CLASSICS/OLYMPICS/TIME TRIALS – 4 POINTS EARNED		
LA FLÈCHE WALLONNE	2	1980
CHAMPIONSHIP OF ZURICH/ZÜRI-METZGETE	2	1979
SEMI-CLASSICS/NATIONALS – 11 POINTS EARNED		
ITALIAN NATIONAL RR CHAMPIONSHIPS	1	1980
GRAND PRIX OF AARGAU CANTON/GP GIPPENGEN	1	1979
GIRO DELLA ROMAGNA	1	1981
MILANO-TORINO/MILAN-TURIN	1	1982
TRE VALLE VARESINE	1	1977, 1979, 1980, 1988
GIRO DEL VENETO	1	1977
TROFEO BARACCHI	1	1979 (WITH FRANCESCO MOSER), 1986 (WITH LECH PIASECKI)

ADDITIONAL GIUSEPPE SARONNI CONTINUED ON THE NEXT PAGE...

RACE	POINTS	YEARS
MINOR TOURS AND STAGE RACES - 20 POINTS EARNED		
TIRRENO-ADRIATICO	3	1978, 1982
TOUR OF ROMANDY	3	1979
TOUR OF SWITZERLAND/TOUR DE SUISSE	3	1982
GIRO DI SARDEGNA	2	1982, 1986
TOUR OF THE ALPS/GIRO DEL TRENTINO	2	1982
GP MIDI LIBRE	2	1979
GRAND TOURS (VARIOUS POINTS) - 16 POINTS EARNED		
GIRO D'ITALIA		
1ST PLACE	6	1979, 1983
2ND PLACE	3	1986
3RD PLACE	1	1981
GRAND TOUR CLASSIFICATION JERSEYS - 8 POINTS EARNED		
GIRO D'ITALIA: POINTS	2	1979, 1980, 1981, 1983
GRAND TOUR STAGE WINS - 14.5 POINTS EARNED		
GIRO D'ITALIA: 24 STAGES, 3 TTT	½ POINT	1978-1988
VUELTA A ESPAÑA: 2 STAGES	½ POINT	1983
SEASON-LONG COMPETITIONS - 0 POINTS EARNED		
HOUR RECORD - 0 POINTS EARNED		
RACE RECORDS (VARIOUS POINTS) - 0 POINTS EARNED		
LIFETIME ACHIEVEMENTS (VARIOUS POINTS) - 0 POINTS EARNED		

Rank 21: Alberto Contador

BORN: **DECEMBER 6, 1982**
YEARS ACTIVE: **2003-2017**
COUNTRY: **SPAIN**
NICKNAME: *EL PISTOLERO*
(THE SHOOTER)

CAREER WINS: **70**
TOTAL POINTS: **84.5**
RAW SCORE: **74.5**

ASIDE FROM LANCE ARMSTRONG, NOBODY HAS SEEN MORE POINTS REMOVED DUE TO A PENALTY from a doping infraction than Alberto Contador. The trace amounts of clenbuterol found in his urine sample from a rest day in the 2010 Tour caused him to lose the points from the victory in that race—Andy Schlek was eventually declared the official winner. Contador also had to have his victory in the 2011 Giro expunged, a race in which he was allowed to participate as his case worked its way through the Court of Arbitration for Sport (CAS). He lost twenty-nine points in this system—not just the ones removed from winning the 2010 Tour and 2011 Giro, but also the fifteen bonus points he would have received by joining Merckx, Anquetil, and Hinault as another eight-time Grand Tour winner.

Despite the huge point losses, he still managed to accrue enough to finish in twenty-first place. Over a seven-year stretch, it was only Eddy Merckx who was a more prolific Grand Tour winner than *El*

Pistolero, and he was the first to have won all three GTs three times. His official *palmarès* include two Tour de France victories, two Giro, three Vuelta, eight Minor Tours, one Semi-Classic, nine Grand Tour stages, and one season-long competition.

RACE	POINTS	YEARS
THE MONUMENTS - 0 POINTS EARNED		
WORLD CHAMPIONSHIP ROAD RACE - 0 POINTS EARNED		
CLASSICS/OLYMPICS/TIME TRIALS - 0 POINTS EARNED		
SEMI-CLASSICS/NATIONALS - 1 POINT EARNED		
MILANO-TORINO/MILAN-TURIN	1	2012
MINOR TOURS AND STAGE RACES - 23 POINTS EARNED		
PARIS-NICE	3	2007, 2010
TIRRENO-ADRIATICO	3	2014
TOUR OF THE BASQUE COUNTRY/VUELTA CICLISTA AL PAIS VASCO	3	2008, 2009, 2014, 2016
CATALAN WEEK/SETMANA CATALUNYA	2	2005
GRAND TOURS (VARIOUS POINTS) - 43 POINTS EARNED		
GIRO D'ITALIA		
1ST PLACE	6	2008, 2015
TOUR DE FRANCE		
1ST PLACE	8	2007, 2009
VUELTA A ESPAÑA (TOUR OF SPAIN)		
1ST PLACE (1974-PRESENT)	5	2008, 2012, 2014
GRAND TOUR CLASSIFICATION JERSEYS - 0 POINTS EARNED		

ADDITIONAL ALBERTO CONTADOR CONTINUED ON THE NEXT PAGE...

RACE	POINTS	YEARS
GRAND TOUR STAGE WINS – 5.5 POINTS EARNED		
TOUR DE FRANCE: 3 STAGES, 1 TTT	½ POINT	2007-2009
VUELTA A ESPAÑA: 7 STAGES	½ POINT	2008-2017
SEASON-LONG COMPETITIONS – 2 POINTS EARNED		
UCI WORLD TOUR ('09-PRESENT)	2	2009
HOUR RECORD - 0 POINTS EARNED		
RACE RECORDS (VARIOUS POINTS) – 0 POINTS EARNED		
LIFETIME ACHIEVEMENTS (VARIOUS POINTS) – 10 POINTS EARNED		
WON ALL THREE GRAND TOURS: 10 POINTS		

Rank 22: Joop Zoetemelk

BORN: **DECEMBER 3, 1946**
YEARS ACTIVE: **1970–1987**
COUNTRY: **NETHERLANDS**
NICKNAME:
THE ETERNAL RUNNER UP

CAREER WINS: **97**
TOTAL POINTS: **84**
RAW SCORE: **84**

ZOETEMELK IS THE NETHERLANDS TOP-RANKED CYCLIST. It's unfortunate that the nickname most associated with the Dutch cyclist is perhaps the most unfair—"The Eternal Runner-Up"—since he did in fact win the Tour de France in 1980, and the Tour of Spain in 1979. He does own the record for most second-place finishes in the Tour—six, which is three more than "The Eternal Second," Raymond Poulidor. Zoetemelk had the unfortunate luck of turning pro right when Merckx was entering his peak years, and then when he retired, Bernard Hinault had arrived on the scene; Zoetemelk's career was sandwiched in between two of the greatest Grand Tour riders in the history of the sport.

He had a horrible crash in the 1974 Midi Libre that nearly cost him his life—he suffered a traumatic head injury when he collided with a misplaced car at the finish line. He obviously missed that year's Tour, but it was Zoetemelk's only absence from the race over the course of his seventeen-year career. Not only did Joop enter sixteen Tours, but he finished all those that he started, a record he shares with Sylvain Chavanel. Zoetemelk also holds the distinction of being the oldest rider to win the World Championship Road Race. He did this at the age of thirty-eight, three months shy of his thirty-ninth birthday. In the closing kilometers, he got the jump on a group in the 1985 race that contained none other than Greg LeMond, Moreno Argentin, and Stephen Roche. That was the exploit of a legendary champion, hardly an eternal runner-up. Zoetemelk also holds the honor of being the first to wear the iconic polka-dot jersey in Tour de France, although it was Lucien Van Impe who actually went on to win the mountains classification in that 1975 edition of the race.

RACE	POINTS	YEARS
THE MONUMENTS – 0 POINTS EARNED		
WORLD CHAMPIONSHIP ROAD RACE – 4 POINTS EARNED		
GOLD	4	1985
CLASSICS/OLYMPICS/TIME TRIALS – 8 POINTS EARNED		
AMSTEL GOLD	2	1987
LA FLÈCHE WALLONNE	2	1976
PARIS–TOURS	2	1977, 1979
SEMI-CLASSICS/NATIONALS – 4 POINTS EARNED		
NETHERLAND NATIONAL RR CHAMPIONSHIPS	1	1971, 1973
CRITÉRIUM DES AS	1	1979, 1980

ADDITIONAL JOOP ZOETEMELK CONTINUED ON THE NEXT PAGE...

RACE	POINTS	YEARS
MINOR TOURS AND STAGE RACES – 21 POINTS EARNED		
PARIS-NICE	3	1974, 1975, 1979
TIRRENO–ADRIATICO	3	1985
TOUR OF ROMANDY	3	1974
CRITÉRIUM INTERNATIONAL	2	1979
CATALAN WEEK/SETMANA CATALUNYA	2	1974
BINCKBANK TOUR/ENECO TOUR OF BENELUX/RONDE VAN NEDERLANDS	2	1975
GRAND TOURS (VARIOUS POINTS) – 37 POINTS EARNED		
TOUR DE FRANCE		
1ST PLACE	8	1980
2ND PLACE	4	1970, 1971, 1976, 1978, 1979, 1982
VUELTA A ESPAÑA (TOUR OF SPAIN)		
1ST PLACE	5	1979
GRAND TOUR CLASSIFICATION JERSEYS – 2 POINTS EARNED		
VUELTA A ESPAÑA: MOUNTAINS	2	1971
GRAND TOUR STAGE WINS – 8 POINTS EARNED		
TOUR DE FRANCE: 10 STAGES, 3 TTT	½ POINT	1973-1983
VUELTA A ESPAÑA: 3 STAGES	½ POINT	1971-1979
SEASON-LONG COMPETITIONS – 0 POINTS EARNED		
HOUR RECORD - 0 POINTS EARNED		
RACE RECORDS (VARIOUS POINTS) – 0 POINTS EARNED		
LIFETIME ACHIEVEMENTS (VARIOUS POINTS) – 0 POINTS EARNED		

Rank 23: Vincenzo Nibali

BORN: **NOVEMBER 14, 1984**
YEARS ACTIVE: **2005–PRESENT**
COUNTRY: **ITALY**
NICKNAME:
LO SQUALO **(THE SHARK)**

CAREER WINS: **55**
TOTAL POINTS: **82**
RAW SCORE: **72**

WHEN NIBALI WON THE 2018 MILAN SAN-REMO, he became
the seventh Italian cyclist to make the Top 25. As of 2019, "The
Shark" is still going strong. He is a bit of throwback to earlier eras,
competing year-round and winning big in both single-day races and
Grand Tours. He has won both Milan-San Remo and the Giro di
Lombardia (twice), was twice the National Road Race Champion,
captured four Minor Tours, won three Semi-Classics, finished on
eleven Grand Tour podiums (including eighteen stage wins), and
most significantly, he is one of seven other cyclists to have won all
three Grand Tours. Although he seems to be past his best years in
the GTs, it wouldn't surprise me if he reached peak form at just the
right time and had another victory in his legs. In this recent age of
specialization, he is the rare complete cyclist, and I'd like to see
him pad his *palmarès* in his last few seasons. If there had been extra
points awarded for insane descending skills, Nibali would certainly
have received them. It could be argued that his win in the 2015 Giro
di Lombardia was primarily due to his downhill gymnastics on the
descent of the Civiglio in that year's race; it's definitely worth looking
up on YouTube.

RACE	POINTS	YEARS
THE MONUMENTS – 9 POINTS EARNED		
MILAN–SAN REMO:	3	2018
IL LOMBARDIA/GIRO DI LOMBARDIA	3	2015, 2017
WORLD CHAMPIONSHIP ROAD RACE – 0 POINTS EARNED		
CLASSICS/OLYMPICS/TIME TRIALS – 0 POINTS EARNED		
SEMI-CLASSICS/NATIONALS – 5 POINTS EARNED		
ITALIAN NATIONAL RR CHAMPIONSHIPS	1	2014, 2015
BRETAGNE CLASSIC OUEST-FRANCE/GP OUEST-FRANCE/ GRAND PRIX DE PLOUAY	1	2006
GIRO DELLA TOSCANA	1	2007
TRE VALLE VARESINE	1	2015
MINOR TOURS AND STAGE RACES – 10 POINTS EARNED		
TIRRENO–ADRIATICO	3	2012, 2013
TOUR OF THE ALPS/GIRO DEL TRENTINO	2	2008, 2013
GRAND TOURS (VARIOUS POINTS) - 39 POINTS EARNED		
GIRO D'ITALIA		
1ST PLACE	6	2013, 2016
2ND PLACE	3	2011, 2019
3RD PLACE	1	2010, 2017
TOUR DE FRANCE		
1ST PLACE	8	2014
3RD PLACE	2	2012
VUELTA A ESPAÑA (TOUR OF SPAIN)		
1ST PLACE	5	2010
2ND PLACE	2	2013, 2017

ADDITIONAL VINCENZO NIBALI CONTINUED ON THE NEXT PAGE...

RACE	POINTS	YEARS
GRAND TOUR CLASSIFICATION JERSEYS - 0 POINTS EARNED		
GRAND TOUR STAGE WINS – 9 POINTS EARNED		
GIRO D'ITALIA: 7 STAGES, 2 TTT	½ POINT	2007-2017
TOUR DE FRANCE: 6 STAGES	½ POINT	2014-2019
VUELTA A ESPAÑA: 2 STAGES, 1 TTT	½ POINT	2010-2017
SEASON-LONG COMPETITIONS – 0 POINTS EARNED		
HOUR RECORD - 0 POINTS EARNED		
RACE RECORDS (VARIOUS POINTS) – 0 POINTS EARNED		
LIFETIME ACHIEVEMENTS (VARIOUS POINTS) – 10 POINTS EARNED		
WON ALL THREE GRAND TOURS: 10 POINTS		

Rank 24: Erik Zabel

BORN: **JULY 7, 1970**
YEARS ACTIVE: **1992–2008**
COUNTRY: **GERMANY**
NICKNAME: *ETE*

CAREER WINS: **144**
TOTAL POINTS: **76**
RAW SCORE: **66**

ZABEL IS GERMANY'S HIGHEST-RANKED CYCLIST, a gifted sprinter whose points were amassed by his remarkable consistency, especially during Grand Tours. He owns the record for most points classification victories at nine, with six of those coming in consecutive years in the Tour de France from 1996 to 2002. What is remarkable is that his actual victory count during that run only totaled twelve stages; not exactly the high count you'd expect. In fact, he won two of those green jerseys without actually winning a stage in 1998 and 1999. Zabel's formula for success was quite simple—he'd consistently finish near the head of the bunch in sprint stages, then solidify his advantage when other sprinters of the day faltered in the mountains and dropped out of the race or missed the time cut. Although not a gifted climber, *Ete* was always able to survive the high mountain stages, not letting the steep gradients ruin his chance of securing another points competition.

He also won the Vuelta points classification three years in a row, from 2002 to 2004. In similar fashion to his string of Tour successes, he secured two of those classifications without winning a stage in 2002 and 2004. Over his career he would capture twenty Grand

Tour stages, but if we include all stage races, he crossed the line first an impressive 114 times.

Zabel won the one Monument best suited to a man of his abilities, Milan-San Remo, four times. He would have won a fifth had he not taken his hands off of the bars for a premature victory salute in 2004, which lead to him getting pipped at the line by Óscar Freire. Paris-Tours was another race that was right in Zabel's wheelhouse, and he took the spoils in that event in 1994, 2003, and 2005. As another testament to his amazing consistency, *Ete* won three season-long competitions three years in a row, from 2000 to 2002.

RACE	POINTS	YEARS
THE MONUMENTS – 12 POINTS EARNED		
MILAN–SAN REMO:	3	1997, 1998, 2000, 2001
WORLD CHAMPIONSHIP ROAD RACE - 5 POINTS EARNED		
SILVER	2	2004, 2006
BRONZE	1	2002
CLASSICS/OLYMPICS/TIME TRIALS – 8 POINTS EARNED		
AMSTEL GOLD	2	2000
PARIS-TOURS	2	1994, 2003, 2005
SEMI-CLASSICS/NATIONALS – 7 POINTS EARNED		
GERMAN NATIONAL RR CHAMPIONSHIPS	1	1998, 2003
SCHELDEPRIJS/GP DE L'ESCAUT/GROTE SCHELDEPRIJS/ SCHELDEPRIJS VLAANDEREN	1	1997
ESCHBORN-FRANKFURT/FRANKFURT GRAND PRIX/RUND UM DEN HENNINGER-TURN	1	1999, 2002, 2005
EUROEYES CYCLASSICS/VATTENFALL CYCLASSICS, HEW CYCLASSICS	1	2001
MINOR TOURS AND STAGE RACES – 0 POINTS EARNED		
GRAND TOURS (VARIOUS POINTS) - 0 POINTS EARNED		

ADDITIONAL ERIK ZABEL CONTINUED ON THE NEXT PAGE...

RACE	POINTS	YEARS
GRAND TOUR CLASSIFICATION JERSEYS – 18 POINTS EARNED		
TOUR DE FRANCE: POINTS	2	1996, 1997, 1998, 1999, 2000, 2001
VUELTA A ESPAÑA: POINTS	2	2002, 2003, 2004
GRAND TOUR STAGE WINS – 10 POINTS EARNED		
TOUR DE FRANCE: 12 STAGES	½ POINT	1995-2002
VUELTA A ESPAÑA: 8 STAGES	½ POINT	2001-2007
SEASON-LONG COMPETITIONS – 6 POINTS EARNED		
UCI ROAD WORLD CUP	2	2000
UCI ROAD WORLD ROAD RANKINGS	2	2001, 2002
HOUR RECORD - 0 POINTS EARNED		
RACE RECORDS (VARIOUS POINTS) – 0 POINTS EARNED		
LIFETIME ACHIEVEMENTS (VARIOUS POINTS) – 10 POINTS EARNED		
WON ANY EIGHT GRAND TOUR CLASSIFICATION JERSEYS: 10 POINTS		

Rank 25: Tom Boonen

BORN: **OCTOBER 15, 1980**
YEARS ACTIVE: **2002-2017**
COUNTRY: **BELGIUM**
NICKNAME: *TOMMEKE /*
TORNADO TOM

CAREER WINS: **121**
TOTAL POINTS: **76**
RAW SCORE: **59**

BOONEN IS ARGUABLY THE GREATEST COBBLED SPRING CLASSICS SPECIALIST ON THIS LIST. Tommeke is the only cyclist who holds the race record for most wins in both cobbled spring Monuments, Flanders and Roubaix; he shares the first with five other cyclists and Roubaix with only Roger De Vlaeminck. In 2005 "Tornado Tom" became the first cyclist able to capture Flanders, Paris-Roubaix, and the World Championship in the same year; unbelievably, a feat that hadn't been accomplished by even the great Eddy Merckx. Along with Johan Museeuw, his childhood idol, they are the only cyclists in the past 40 years to amass 25 wins in all single-day races in this scoring system; Francesco Moser had accomplished the rare combination of victories back in 1979.

The last handful of Boonen's seasons were marred by crashes, which often resulted in extended periods of downtime. He nearly lost his arm to amputation in early 2013 after developing a horrible infection from an elbow wound. Despite a terrible crash in late 2015 that knocked him unconscious and left him with permanent damage to his hearing, he came back and nearly won the 2016 Paris-Roubaix, just losing the two-up sprint to the line to Matthew Hayman. You have to wonder how much more Tornado Tom would have won had he not had such misfortune at the tail end of his career.

RACE	POINTS	YEARS
THE MONUMENTS – 25 POINTS EARNED		
TOUR OF FLANDERS/RONDE VAN VLAANDEREN	3	2005, 2006, 2012
PARIS-ROUBAIX	4	2005, 2008, 2009, 2012
WORLD CHAMPIONSHIP ROAD RACE - 5 POINTS EARNED		
GOLD	4	2005
BRONZE	1	2016
CLASSICS/OLYMPICS/TIME TRIALS - 6 POINTS EARNED		
GHENT-WEVELGEM	2	2004, 2011, 2012
SEMI-CLASSICS/NATIONALS – 15 POINTS EARNED		
BELGIAN NATIONAL RR CHAMPIONSHIPS	1	2009, 2012
KUURNE–BRUSSELS–KUURNE	1	2007, 2009, 2014
DWARS DOOR VLAANDEREN	1	2007
E3 BINKBANK CLASSIC/E3 HARELBEKE/HARELBEKE-ANT-WERP–HARELBEKE/E3 PRIJS VLAANDEREN	1	2004, 2005, 2006, 2007, 2012
SCHELDEPRIJS/GP DE L'ESCAUT/GROTE SCHELDEPRIJS/ SCHELDEPRIJS VLAANDEREN	1	2004, 2006
BRUSSELS CYCLING CLASSIC/PARIS-BRUSSELS	1	2012, 2016
MINOR TOURS AND STAGE RACES - 2 POINTS EARNED		
TOUR OF BELGIUM	2	2005
GRAND TOURS (VARIOUS POINTS) - 0 POINTS EARNED		

ADDITIONAL TOM BOONEN CONTINUED ON THE NEXT PAGE...

RACE	POINTS	YEARS
GRAND TOUR CLASSIFICATION JERSEYS – 2 POINTS EARNED		
TOUR DE FRANCE: POINTS	2	2007
GRAND TOUR STAGE WINS - 4 POINTS EARNED		
TOUR DE FRANCE: 6 STAGES	½ POINT	2004-2007
VUELTA A ESPAÑA: 2 STAGES	½ POINT	2008
SEASON-LONG COMPETITIONS – 0 POINTS EARNED		
HOUR RECORD - 0 POINTS EARNED		
RACE RECORDS (VARIOUS POINTS) – 7 POINTS EARNED		
TOUR OF FLANDERS: 3 POINTS (SHARED WITH ACHIEL BUYSSE, FIORENZO MAGNI, ERIC LEMAN, JOHAN MUSEEUW, AND FABIAN CANCELLARA)		
PARIS-ROUBAIX: 4 POINTS (SHARED WITH ROGER DE VLAEMINCK)		
LIFETIME ACHIEVEMENTS (VARIOUS POINTS) – 10 POINTS EARNED		
25 COMBINED WINS IN ALL MAJOR SINGLE-DAY RACES: 10 PTS		

Rank 26: Rik Van Steenbergen

BORN: **SEPTEMBER 9, 1924**
YEARS ACTIVE: **1943-1966**
COUNTRY: **BELGIUM**
NICKNAME: **THE BOSS / RIK I**

CAREER WINS: **63**
TOTAL POINTS: **73.5**
RAW SCORE: **62.5**

WHEN I LOOK AT HIS SCORING SHEET, THE FIRST THING I'M STRUCK BY IS WHAT A LONG CAREER HE HAD, which spanned a twenty-four-year period from 1942 to 1966—World War II all the way to the Vietnam War. I think it's safe to say many others would have called it quits long before Van Steenbergen did, as his last professional victory was in March 1961, more than five years before his retirement. The final points he earned in this scoring system were in 1958's Critérium des As. The other thing I'm struck by is that even during his heyday, he only captured one Belgian Semi-Classic, the 1945 Dwars Door Vlaanderen. It's an odd contrast to the other Belgian single-day specialists ahead of him on this list.

It is of course unfair to simply look at the races Van Steenbergen didn't win. "The Boss" earned that nickname for a good reason—during his prime years, from the mid-1940s to the mid-'50s, he won three World Championship RR titles, five Monuments, three Classics, and twenty-five Grand Tour stages. In a striking contrast to those one-day races, Van Steenbergen would vie for victory in the 1951 Giro, where he finished second overall, only 1 minute, 46 seconds behind winner Fiorenzo Magni. Incredibly, a cyclist not known for his climbing ability, he finished ahead of a veritable who's who of postwar Grand Tour legends—Ferdi Kübler, Fausto Coppi, Hugo Koblet, Louison Bobet, and Gino Bartali. Yes, unbelievably, they were all in that race, conceivably the greatest Giro lineup in its history. We are left to wonder if Van Steenbergen might have had a completely different career trajectory had he actually focused on developing his climbing abilities. Although not included in this system, Van Steenbergen was a prolific track winner, amassing an incredible forty Six Day victories, as well as nine Belgian and six European track titles.

RACE	POINTS	YEARS
THE MONUMENTS – 17 POINTS EARNED		
MILAN–SAN REMO:	3	1954
TOUR OF FLANDERS/RONDE VAN VLAANDEREN	3	1944, 1946
PARIS-ROUBAIX	4	1948, 1952
WORLD CHAMPIONSHIP ROAD RACE – 13 POINTS EARNED		
GOLD	4	1949, 1956, 1957
BRONZE	1	1946
CLASSICS/OLYMPICS/TIME TRIALS – 6 POINTS EARNED		
LA FLÈCHE WALLONNE	2	1949, 1948
PARIS-BRUSSELS	2	1950
SEMI-CLASSICS/NATIONALS – 9 POINTS EARNED		
BELGIAN NATIONAL RR CHAMPIONSHIPS	1	1943, 1945, 1954
DWARS DOOR VLAANDEREN	1	1945
CRITÉRIUM DES AS	1	1948, 1952, 1955, 1957, 1958
MINOR TOURS AND STAGE RACES – 0 POINTS EARNED		

ADDITIONAL RIK VAN STEENBERGEN CONTINUED ON THE NEXT PAGE...

RACE	POINTS	YEARS
GRAND TOURS (VARIOUS POINTS) - 3 POINTS EARNED		
GIRO D'ITALIA		
2ND PLACE	3	1951
GRAND TOUR CLASSIFICATION JERSEYS – 2 POINTS EARNED		
VUELTA A ESPAÑA: POINTS	2	1956
GRAND TOUR STAGE WINS – 12.5 POINTS EARNED		
GIRO D'ITALIA: 15 STAGES	½ POINT	1951-1957
TOUR DE FRANCE: 4 STAGES	½ POINT	1949-1955
VUELTA A ESPAÑA: 6 STAGES	½ POINT	1956
SEASON-LONG COMPETITIONS – 0 POINTS EARNED		
HOUR RECORD - 0 POINTS EARNED		
RACE RECORDS (VARIOUS POINTS) - 4 POINTS EARNED		
WORLD CHAMPIONSHIP ROAD RACE: 4 POINTS (SHARED WITH ALFREDO BINDA, EDDY MERCKX, ÓSCAR FREIRE, AND PETER SAGAN)		
LIFETIME ACHIEVEMENTS (VARIOUS POINTS) – 7 POINTS EARNED		
MISSING YEARS ADJUSTMENT: 7 POINTS		

Rank 27: Mario Cipollini

BORN: **MARCH 22, 1967**
YEARS ACTIVE: **1989–2005**
COUNTRY: **ITALY**
NICKNAME: **CIPO / THE LION KING**

CAREER WINS: **167**
TOTAL POINTS: **73.5**
RAW SCORE: **53.5**

"SUPER MARIO" CAN BE CREDITED WITH CREATING THE MODERN SPRINT TRAIN. Sure, there are other sprinters ahead of him on this list, but he was the first to have an entire team at his disposal with the sole goal of keeping the pace extremely high, protecting their leader, and putting him in the best position to launch for the line. That sprint train was never more evident than at the Giro; "Cipo" broke Alfredo Binda's stage win record, set all the way back in 1933, with his forty-second win in Italy's Grand Tour in 2003. It's no surprise that he also won the points classification in that race three times, in 1992, 1997, and 2002. After Merckx, Cipollini has the most road victories in this scoring system.*

Although he also won twelve Tour de France stages and three in the Vuelta, both of those races were routinely abandoned in the

---

*As mentioned at the beginning Part IV, I have chosen to use only professional road race victories and time trials in this scoring system. If we are to include amateur, track, criterium, kermesse, six-day competitions, as well as points and mountains classifications and season-long competitions as wins, then overall victory counts look quite different for many cyclists.

mountains, where Cipollini made it very clear he had no interest suffering in the *grupetto*.* Although almost as famous for his outlandish clothing and flamboyant lifestyle as he was for his sprinting prowess, the "Lion King" was a gifted cyclist who also won Milan-San Remo, the World Championship RR gold medal, and three Ghent-Wevelgem.

---

*Grupetto is the Italian term for the French autobus, which is the group that forms at the back of the race during mountain stages. They work together in order to avoid elimination due to missing the daily time cut. Also known as "the laughing group," due to their comradery in getting through tough stages ill-suited for their talents, they often share food and drinks even though they might be on different teams.

RACE	POINTS	YEARS
THE MONUMENTS – 3 POINTS EARNED		
MILAN–SAN REMO:	3	2002
WORLD CHAMPIONSHIP ROAD RACE - 4 POINTS EARNED		
GOLD	4	2002
CLASSICS/OLYMPICS/TIME TRIALS – 6 POINTS EARNED		
GHENT–WEVELGEM	2	1992, 1993, 2002
SEMI-CLASSICS/NATIONALS – 4 POINTS EARNED		
ITALIAN NATIONAL RR CHAMPIONSHIPS	1	1996
E3 BINKBANK CLASSIC/E3 HARELBEKE/ HARELBEKE–ANTWERP–HARELBEKE/E3 PRIJS VLAANDEREN	1	1993
SCHELDEPRIJS/GP DE L'ESCAUT/GROTE SCHELDEPRIJS/ SCHELDEPRIJS VLAANDEREN	1	1991, 1993
MINOR TOURS AND STAGE RACES - 2 POINTS EARNED		
FOUR DAYS OF DUNKIRK	2	1992
GRAND TOURS (VARIOUS POINTS) - 0 POINTS EARNED		

ADDITIONAL MARIO CIPOLLINI CONTINUED ON THE NEXT PAGE...

RACE	POINTS	YEARS
GRAND TOUR CLASSIFICATION JERSEYS – 6 POINTS EARNED		
GIRO D'ITALIA: POINTS	2	1992, 1997, 2002
GRAND TOUR STAGE WINS – 28.5 POINTS EARNED		
GIRO D'ITALIA: 42 STAGE WINS (RECORD)	½ POINT	1989-2003
TOUR DE FRANCE: 12 STAGES	½ POINT	1993-1999
VUELTA A ESPAÑA: 3 STAGES	½ POINT	2002
SEASON-LONG COMPETITIONS – 0 POINTS EARNED		
HOUR RECORD – 0 POINTS EARNED		
RACE RECORDS (VARIOUS POINTS) – 0 POINTS EARNED		
LIFETIME ACHIEVEMENTS (VARIOUS POINTS) – 20 POINTS EARNED		
WON 30 GRAND TOUR STAGES: 10 PTS		
WON 150 OR MORE PROFESSIONAL ROAD RACES: 10 POINTS		

Rank 28: Raymond Poulidor

BORN: **APRIL 15, 1936**
YEARS ACTIVE: **1960-1977**
COUNTRY: **FRANCE**
NICKNAME: *POUPOU* /
THE ETERNAL SECOND

CAREER WINS: **73**
TOTAL POINTS: **70.5**
RAW SCORE: **70.5**

POULIDOR WAS A GIFTED ALL-ROUNDER, BUT LIKE JOOP ZOETEMELK, ALSO HAD THE MISFORTUNE of having to compete against two of the greatest Grand Tour champions in history. At the front half of his career it was Jacques Anquetil and during the second half it was Eddy Merckx. It should come as no surprise that Poulidor became known as "The Eternal Second." Although like Zoetemelk, Poulidor didn't always finish second, since he did win the 1964 Vuelta. "Pou-Pou" had a long career and was competitive throughout, turning pro with Mercier in 1960 and retiring with the same team in 1977.

As a testament to his longevity, he won Milan-San Remo in 1961, and at the age of forty in 1976, placed third in the Tour de France. In between those years he won La Flèche Wallone, the Grand Prix de Nations, the Critérium des As, the French National RR Championship, five editions of the Critérium National, six Minor Tours, eleven Grand Tour stages, and the 1964 Super Prestige Pernod Trophy. In total, he finished on the podium in the Tour de France eight times, with three second and five third places, but unbelievably never once wore the yellow jersey—not even for a single day. The cycling gods can be a cruel lot.

RACE	POINTS	YEARS
THE MONUMENTS – 3 POINTS EARNED		
MILAN–SAN REMO:	3	1961
WORLD CHAMPIONSHIP ROAD RACE - 5 POINTS EARNED		
SILVER	2	1974
BRONZE	1	1961, 1964, 1966
CLASSICS/OLYMPICS/TIME TRIALS – 4 POINTS EARNED		
LA FLÈCHE WALLONNE	2	1963
GRAND PRIX DE NATIONS	2	1963
SEMI-CLASSICS/NATIONALS – 7 POINTS EARNED		
FRENCH NATIONAL RR CHAMPIONSHIPS	1	1961
CRITÉRIUM NATIONAL DE LA ROUTE	1	1964, 1966, 1968, 1971, 1972
CRITÉRIUM DES AS	1	1972
MINOR TOURS AND STAGE RACES – 16 POINTS EARNED		
PARIS-NICE	3	1972, 1973
CRITÉRIUM DU DAUPHINÉ/CRITÉRIUM DU DAUPHINÉ LIBÉRÉ	3	1966, 1969
CATALAN WEEK/SETMANA CATALUNYA	2	1971
GP MIDI LIBRE	2	1973
GRAND TOURS (VARIOUS POINTS) - 28 POINTS EARNED		
TOUR DE FRANCE		
2ND PLACE	4	1964, 1965, 1974
3RD PLACE	2	1962, 1966, 1969, 1972, 1976
VUELTA A ESPAÑA (TOUR OF SPAIN)		
1ST PLACE (PRE 1974)	4	1964
2ND PLACE	2	1967
GRAND TOUR CLASSIFICATION JERSEYS – 0 POINTS EARNED		

ADDITIONAL RAYMOND POULIDOR CONTINUED ON THE NEXT PAGE...

RACE	POINTS	YEARS
GRAND TOUR STAGE WINS – 5.5 POINTS EARNED		
TOUR DE FRANCE: 7 STAGES	½ POINT	1962-1974
VUELTA A ESPAÑA: 4 STAGES	½ POINT	1964-1965
SEASON-LONG COMPETITIONS – 2 POINTS EARNED		
SUPER PRESTIGE PERNOD TROPHY	2	1964
HOUR RECORD - 0 POINTS EARNED		
RACE RECORDS (VARIOUS POINTS) – 0 POINTS EARNED		
LIFETIME ACHIEVEMENTS (VARIOUS POINTS) – 0 POINTS EARNED		

Rank 29: Johan Museeuw

BORN: **OCTOBER 13, 1965**
YEARS ACTIVE: **1988–2004**
COUNTRY: **BELGIUM**
NICKNAME: **THE LION OF FLANDERS /**
DE ZEEMEEUW **(THE SEAGULL)**

CAREER WINS: **68**
TOTAL POINTS: **70**
RAW SCORE: **57**

MUSEEUW WAS A PROLIFIC WINNER. In 2003 he captured twenty-five single-day races in this scoring system, the first to do so since Francesco Moser in 1979, a long 24 year gap. The second "Lion of Flanders" after Fiorenzo Magni, Museeuw earned that nickname by virtue of his three Flanders victories in 1993, 1995, and 1998. In addition to his Flanders triumphs, he also won Paris-Roubaix three times (1996, 2000, and 2002), at the time becoming the first rider to win both races three times. His protégé, Tom Boonen, would match that feat and go one better by adding a fourth Paris-Roubaix to his *palmarès*.

In addition to his cobbled Monument conquests, Museeuw also claimed the World Championship RR gold medal in 1996, two season-long competitions in 1995 and 1996 (UCI World Cup), two editions of Zuri-Metzgete (1991 and 1995), Paris-Tours in 1993, the 1994 Amstel Gold, and numerous cobbled Semi-Classics. Museeuw was a tenacious competitor, twice coming back from potential career-ending injuries. One week after his 1998 Flanders victory, he crashed heavily during one of the cobbled sectors in Paris-Roubaix, shattering his knee cap. The knee later became infected, and he almost lost his leg to amputation, yet he fought back from the injury to win Paris-Roubaix in 2000. Later that same year, he suffered a traumatic head injury in a motorcycle accident, spending days in a coma. Again, he fought back from an injury that surely would have caused most to retire from the sport, winning his third and final Paris-Roubaix in 2002—a true Belgian hardman.

RACE	POINTS	YEARS
THE MONUMENTS – 21 POINTS EARNED		
TOUR OF FLANDERS/RONDE VAN VLAANDEREN	3	1993, 1995, 1998
PARIS-ROUBAIX	4	1996, 2000, 2002
WORLD CHAMPIONSHIP ROAD RACE - 4 POINTS EARNED		
GOLD	4	1996
CLASSICS/OLYMPICS/TIME TRIALS – 8 POINTS EARNED		
AMSTEL GOLD	2	1994
PARIS-TOURS	2	1993
CHAMPIONSHIP OF ZURICH/ZURI-METZGETE	2	1991, 1995
SEMI-CLASSICS/NATIONALS – 14 POINTS EARNED		
BELGIAN NATIONAL RR CHAMPIONSHIPS	1	1992, 1996
OMLOOP HET NIEUWSBLAD/HET VOLK	1	2000, 2003
KUURNE-BRUSSELS-KUURNE	1	1994, 1997
DWARS DOOR VLAANDEREN	1	1993, 1999
E3 BINKBANK CLASSIC/E3 HARELBEKE/HARELBEKE-ANT-WERP-HARELBEKE/E3 PRIJS VLAANDEREN	1	1992, 1998
BRABANTSE PIJL/FLÈCHE BRABANÇONNE	1	1996, 1998, 2000
EUROEYES CYCLASSICS/VATTENFALL CYCLASSICS, HEW CYCLASSICS	1	2002

ADDITIONAL JOHAN MUSEEUW CONTINUED ON THE NEXT PAGE...

RACE	POINTS	YEARS
MINOR TOURS AND STAGE RACES – 4 POINTS EARNED		
FOUR DAYS OF DUNKIRK	2	1995, 1997
GRAND TOURS (VARIOUS POINTS) – 0 POINTS EARNED		
GRAND TOUR CLASSIFICATION JERSEYS – 0 POINTS EARNED		
GRAND TOUR STAGE WINS – 2 POINTS EARNED		
TOUR DE FRANCE: 4 STAGES	½ POINT	1990–1994
SEASON-LONG COMPETITIONS – 4 POINTS EARNED		
UCI ROAD WORLD CUP	2	1995, 1996
HOUR RECORD – 0 POINTS EARNED		
RACE RECORDS (VARIOUS POINTS) – 3 POINTS EARNED		
TOUR OF FLANDERS: 3 POINTS (SHARED WITH ACHIEL BUYSSE, FIORENZO MAGNI, ERIC LEMAN, TOM BOONEN, AND FABIAN CANCELLARA)		
LIFETIME ACHIEVEMENTS (VARIOUS POINTS) – 10 POINTS EARNED		
25 COMBINED WINS IN ALL MAJOR SINGLE-DAY RACES: 10 PTS		

Rank 30: Greg LeMond

BORN: **JUNE 26, 1961**
YEARS ACTIVE: **1981-1994**
COUNTRY: **USA**
NICKNAME:
L'AMERICAIN **(THE AMERICAN) /**
LEMONSTER

CAREER WINS: **33**
TOTAL POINTS: **66**
RAW SCORE: **53**

POSSIBLY THE GREATEST WHAT IF ON THIS LIST: What if LeMond hadn't been shot and nearly killed in a hunting accident in the spring of 1987, and what if he hadn't been competing at the dawn of the EPO generation? There is no doubt in my mind that he would have won more. Probably a lot more. Even though he has been credited with an additional thirteen points with the Missing Years Adjustment Formula—the same formula used to compensate Coppi and Bartali for their missing war years—I don't think that the bonus points offset what he was truly capable of winning. I touched on this topic back in the section about doping, but my conviction is that LeMond would have won at least two more Tours in the early '90s, adding to his victories in 1986, 1989, and 1990. I also think that had he not been shot, there's a pretty good chance he'd have won at least one Monument or maybe another World Championship title (to go along with the two from 1983 and 1989).

Many are unaware of how well LeMond performed in some of
the big races outside of Grand Tours—second in the 1983 Giro
di Lombardia, third in the 1984 Liège-Bastogne-Liège, fourth in
the 1985 Paris-Roubaix, and second in the 1986 Milan-San Remo.
LeMond also won the 1983 Super Prestige Pernod Trophy, the year
after Bernard Hinault had won four straight titles and the year
before Sean Kelly won three of them in succession. After 1986 Greg
was never a factor in any of the Classics, although he did win the
World RR title in 1989 and was fourth in that same race in 1990. It's
also worth noting that he finished in third place at the Giro in 1985,
the year before his first Tour win. What could have been. . . .

RACE	POINTS	YEARS
THE MONUMENTS – 0 POINTS EARNED		
WORLD CHAMPIONSHIP ROAD RACE - 12 POINTS EARNED		
GOLD	4	1983, 1989
SILVER	2	1982, 1985
CLASSICS/OLYMPICS/TIME TRIALS – 0 POINTS EARNED		
SEMI-CLASSICS/NATIONALS – 1 POINT EARNED		
CRITÉRIUM DES AS	1	1983
MINOR TOURS AND STAGE RACES – 3 POINTS EARNED		
CRITÉRIUM DU DAUPHINÉ/CRITÉRIUM DU DAUPHINÉ LIBÉRÉ	3	1983

ADDITIONAL GREG LEMOND CONTINUED ON THE NEXT PAGE...

RACE	POINTS	YEARS
GRAND TOURS (VARIOUS POINTS) - 31 POINTS EARNED		
GIRO D'ITALIA		
3RD PLACE	1	1985
TOUR DE FRANCE		
1ST PLACE	8	1986, 1989, 1990
2ND PLACE	4	1985
3RD PLACE	2	1984
GRAND TOUR CLASSIFICATION JERSEYS – 0 POINTS EARNED		
GRAND TOUR STAGE WINS - 4 POINTS EARNED		
GIRO D'ITALIA: 1 STAGE	½ POINT	1986
TOUR DE FRANCE: 5 STAGES, 2 TTT	½ POINT	1984-1989
SEASON-LONG COMPETITIONS – 2 POINTS EARNED		
SUPER PRESTIGE PERNOD TROPHY	2	1983
HOUR RECORD - 0 POINTS EARNED		
RACE RECORDS (VARIOUS POINTS) – 0 POINTS EARNED		
LIFETIME ACHIEVEMENTS (VARIOUS POINTS) – 13 POINTS EARNED		
MISSING YEARS ADJUSTMENT: 13 POINTS		

Rank 31: Peter Sagan

BORN: **JANUARY 26, 1990**
YEARS ACTIVE: **2009–PRESENT**
COUNTRY: **SLOVAKIA**
NICKNAME: **PETO /**
PETER THE GREAT / TOURMINATOR /
THREE-PETE

CAREER WINS: **113**
TOTAL POINTS: **65**
RAW SCORE: **61**

IT COULD BE ARGUED THAT SAGAN IS JUST NOW ENTERING the prime of his career, since he will be turning 30 at the beginning of the 2020 season. Yet, he has already won three World Championships in a row, captured a record setting seven Tour de France green jerseys, won both Flanders and Paris-Roubaix, and has already accumulated 113 career victories (as of year-end 2019). Barring injury or illness, it seems that "Peter the Great" is destined to rocket up the standings, since he is clearly on the path to collecting possibly three of the Career Milestone Adjustments in this system—ten points for twenty-five wins in all single-day races, ten points for winning eight GT classification competitions, and another ten points for 150 career road victories. Milan-San Remo will certainly end up in his win column at some point (he's finished in the top ten seven times), but it's not that farfetched to think that he could shed a little weight and be competitive in both Liège and Lombardia. Along with Philippe Gilbert, I don't see any other current cyclist who could perhaps win all five Monuments.

RACE	POINTS	YEARS
THE MONUMENTS – 7 POINTS EARNED		
TOUR OF FLANDERS/RONDE VAN VLAANDEREN	3	2016
PARIS-ROUBAIX	4	2018
WORLD CHAMPIONSHIP ROAD RACE - 12 POINTS EARNED		
GOLD	4	2015, 2016, 2017
CLASSICS/OLYMPICS/TIME TRIALS – 8 POINTS EARNED		
GHENT–WEVELGEM	2	2013, 2016, 2018
SEMI-CLASSICS/NATIONALS – 8 POINTS EARNED		
CROATIAN NATIONAL RR CHAMPIONSHIPS	1	2011, 2012, 2013, 2014, 2015, 2018
E3 BINKBANK CLASSIC/E3 HARELBEKE/HARELBEKE-ANTWERP-HARELBEKE/E3 PRIJS VLAANDEREN	1	2014
BRABANTSE PIJL/FLÈCHE BRABANÇONNE	1	2013
MINOR TOURS AND STAGE RACES – 0 POINTS EARNED		
GRAND TOURS (VARIOUS POINTS) - 0 POINTS EARNED		
GRAND TOUR CLASSIFICATION JERSEYS – 14 POINTS EARNED		
TOUR DE FRANCE: POINTS (RACE RECORD)	2	2012, 2013, 2014, 2015, 2016, 2018, 2019
GRAND TOUR STAGE WINS – 8 POINTS EARNED		
TOUR DE FRANCE: 12 STAGES	½ POINT	2012-2019
VUELTA A ESPAÑA: 4 STAGES	½ POINT	2011-2015

ADDITIONAL PETER SAGAN CONTINUED ON THE NEXT PAGE...

RACE	POINTS	YEARS
SEASON-LONG COMPETITIONS – 4 POINTS EARNED		
UCI WORLD TOUR	2	2016
UCI WORLD RANKING	2	2016
HOUR RECORD - 0 POINTS EARNED		
RACE RECORDS (VARIOUS POINTS) – 4 POINTS EARNED		
WORLD CHAMPIONSHIP ROAD RACE: 4 POINTS (SHARED WITH ALFREDO BINDA, RIK VAN STEENBERGEN, EDDY MERCKX, AND OSCAR FREIRE)		
LIFETIME ACHIEVEMENTS (VARIOUS POINTS) – 0 POINTS EARNED		

Rank 32: Jan Janssen

BORN: **MAY 19, 1940**
YEARS ACTIVE: **1962–1972**
COUNTRY: **NETHERLANDS**
NICKNAME: **THE PROFESSOR**

CAREER WINS: **46**
TOTAL POINTS: **63**
RAW SCORE: **53**

"THE PROFESSOR"—SO NAMED FOR HIS THICK, HORN-RIMMED GLASSES—was the first Dutch rider to win the Tour de France. He accomplished this in 1968 by sealing victory only at the very end of the race, capturing the last stage time trial and donning the final yellow jersey with a winning margin of only thirty-eight seconds. That would stand as the narrowest winning margin in Tour history until Greg LeMond defeated Laurent Fignon in 1989 by a mere eight seconds. Janssen wasn't a prolific winner but had a knack for winning big races—the Zuri-Metzgete in 1962 (in its heyday considered a race nearly on par with the other Monuments), Paris-Nice in 1964, the World Championship RR in 1964, Paris-Roubaix in 1967, the Vuelta in 1967, and the Tour in 1968. He also won the points competition twice in the Vuelta and three times in the Tour. Over his career he also claimed ten Grand Tour stages—seven in France, three in Spain. Janssen was also the winner of the season-long Super Prestige Pernod Trophy in 1967. Such was the breadth of "The Professor's" wins that he's one of only seven cyclists to have won a race in every road category in this system. I'm sure he's not one of the names that would typically come up when discussing the greatest all-rounders in the sport's history, but his *palmarès* say otherwise.

RACE	POINTS	YEARS
THE MONUMENTS – 4 POINTS EARNED		
PARIS-ROUBAIX	4	1967
WORLD CHAMPIONSHIP ROAD RACE - 6 POINTS EARNED		
GOLD	4	1964
SILVER	2	1967
CLASSICS/OLYMPICS/TIME TRIALS – 4 POINTS EARNED		
CHAMPIONSHIP OF ZURICH/ZÜRI-METZGETE	2	1962
BORDEAUX-PARIS	2	1966
SEMI-CLASSICS/NATIONALS – 1 POINT EARNED		
BRABANTSE PIJL/FLÈCHE BRABANÇONNE	1	1966
MINOR TOURS AND STAGE RACES – 5 POINTS EARNED		
PARIS-NICE	3	1964
BINCKBANK TOUR/ENECO TOUR OF BENELUX/RONDE VAN NEDERLANDS	2	1965
GRAND TOURS (VARIOUS POINTS) - 16 POINTS EARNED		
TOUR DE FRANCE		
1ST PLACE	8	1968
2ND PLACE	4	1966
VUELTA A ESPAÑA (TOUR OF SPAIN)		
1ST PLACE (PRE 1974)	4	1967

ADDITIONAL JAN JANSSEN CONTINUED ON THE NEXT PAGE...

RACE	POINTS	YEARS
GRAND TOUR CLASSIFICATION JERSEYS – 10 POINTS EARNED		
TOUR DE FRANCE: POINTS	2	1964, 1965, 1967
VUELTA A ESPAÑA: POINTS	2	1967, 1968
GRAND TOUR STAGE WINS - 5 POINTS EARNED		
TOUR DE FRANCE: 7 STAGES	½ POINT	1963-1968
VUELTA A ESPAÑA: 3 STAGES	½ POINT	1967-1968
SEASON-LONG COMPETITIONS – 2 POINTS EARNED		
SUPER PRESTIGE PERNOD TROPHY	2	1967
HOUR RECORD - 0 POINTS EARNED		
RACE RECORDS (VARIOUS POINTS) – 0 POINTS EARNED		
LIFETIME ACHIEVEMENTS (VARIOUS POINTS) – 10 POINTS EARNED		
ACHIEVED AT LEAST ONE VICTORY IN EVERY ROAD CATEGORY: 10 POINTS		

Rank 33: Laurent Fignon

BORN: **AUGUST 12, 1960**
YEARS ACTIVE: **1982–1993**
COUNTRY: **FRANCE**
NICKNAME:
LE PROFESSEUR (THE PROFESSOR)

CAREER WINS: **60**
TOTAL POINTS: **62.5**
RAW SCORE: **62.5**

FIGNON IS THE SPORT'S SECOND BESPECTACLED "PROFESSOR"—THE FIRST BEING NETHERLAND'S JAN JANSSEN. After winning the Tour de France two years running in 1983 and 1984, Fignon looked unstoppable, ready to go on a tear and etch his name into the record books—he was on the fast track to joining the all-time greats. In the 1984 edition of the French race he won by a ten-minute cushion, soundly defeating none other than Bernard Hinault, who was at the height of his powers. If a legend such as The Badger could be so easily dispatched, what was stopping Fignon from becoming the greatest Grand Tour cyclist in the history of the sport? He was only twenty-four and had his entire career ahead of him. That 1984 race would prove to be Fignon's last Tour de France victory. After competing in the 1985 Liège-Bastogne-Liège, he was forced to undergo surgery for an injured Achilles tendon and missed the rest of the season. Although Fignon would go on to win the 1986 La Flèche Wallone, two Milan-San Remo (1988 and 1989), and the

1989 Giro, it's safe to say he never regained the dominating form he possessed prior to the injury. Sadly, *Le Professeur* will probably best be remembered for the crushing eight-second loss to Greg LeMond in the 1989 Tour de France, rather than his earlier Tour conquests. Fignon did win that year's season-long competition, at the time the UCI World Rankings—a small token of consolation from the fickle cycling gods.

RACE	POINTS	YEARS
THE MONUMENTS – 6 POINTS EARNED		
MILAN–SAN REMO:	3	1988, 1989
WORLD CHAMPIONSHIP ROAD RACE –0 POINTS EARNED		
CLASSICS/OLYMPICS/TIME TRIALS – 4 POINTS EARNED		
LA FLÈCHE WALLONNE	2	1986
GRAND PRIX DE NATIONS	2	1989
SEMI-CLASSICS/NATIONALS – 3 POINTS EARNED		
FRENCH NATIONAL RR CHAMPIONSHIPS	1	1984
CRITÉRIUM DES AS	1	1989
TROFEO BARACCHI	1	1989
MINOR TOURS AND STAGE RACES – 8 POINTS EARNED		
CRITÉRIUM INTERNATIONAL	2	1982, 1990
SETTIMANA INTERNAZIONALE COPPI E BARTALI/GIRO DI SARDEGNA	2	1985
BINCKBANK TOUR/ENECO TOUR OF BENELUX/RONDE VAN NEDERLANDS	2	1989

ADDITIONAL LAURENT FIGNON CONTINUED ON THE NEXT PAGE...

RACE	POINTS	YEARS
GRAND TOURS (VARIOUS POINTS) - 29 POINTS EARNED		
GIRO D'ITALIA		
1ST PLACE	6	1989
2ND PLACE	3	1984
TOUR DE FRANCE		
1ST PLACE	8	1983, 1984
2ND PLACE	4	1989
GRAND TOUR CLASSIFICATION JERSEYS - 2 POINTS EARNED		
GIRO D'ITALIA: MOUNTAINS	2	1984
GRAND TOUR STAGE WINS - 8.5 POINTS EARNED		
GIRO D'ITALIA: 2 STAGES, 2 TTT	½ POINT	1984-1989
TOUR DE FRANCE: 9 STAGES, 2 TTT	½ POINT	1983-1989
VUELTA A ESPAÑA: 2 STAGES	½ POINT	1983-1987
SEASON-LONG COMPETITIONS - 2 POINTS EARNED		
UCI ROAD WORLD ROAD RANKINGS	2	1989
HOUR RECORD - 0 POINTS EARNED		
RACE RECORDS (VARIOUS POINTS) - 0 POINTS EARNED		
LIFETIME ACHIEVEMENTS (VARIOUS POINTS) - 0 POINTS EARNED		

Rank 34: Luis Ocaña

BORN: **JUNE 9, 1945**
YEARS ACTIVE: **1968-1977**
COUNTRY: **SPAIN**
NICKNAME: *CHEPAS* (HUMPY)

CAREER WINS: **60**
TOTAL POINTS: **59.5**
RAW SCORE: **59.5**

HE WAS THE ONE CYCLIST WHO WAS ACTUALLY ABLE TO PUT A DENT in Eddy Merckx's nearly invincible Grand Tour suit of armor. It happened on stage eleven of the 1971 Tour de France, when Ocaña broke away and unbelievably put nine minutes into a stunned Eddy Merckx during an epic mountain stage before the second rest day. Such was the ferocity of the Spaniard's attack that sixty-one cyclists finished outside of the time limit on that stage, leaving only thirty-nine left in the race; it was one of the greatest performances in Tour history. The race organizers later changed the original cutoff time so that an additional fifty-eight cyclists were able to take the start line for the twelfth stage. Merckx organized a breakaway and took back two minutes during that stage, but Ocaña still held a huge, almost eight-minute cushion. Stage thirteen was a fairly short 16.5 kilometer time trial; Ocaña held his own and still lead by 7 minutes, 23 seconds—the race looked like it was his for the taking. Disaster struck during stage fourteen when Ocaña crashed while descending in the pouring rain, chasing Merckx down the treacherous switchbacks of the Col de Mende. As he got off the ground, Joop Zoetemelk lost control and slammed into him. The helpless Spaniard was then blasted by two more cyclists and was semiconscious and in agonizing pain when he was finally loaded into an ambulance, his bid for Tour glory abruptly cut short. Merckx went on to win the race that year. Ocaña did eventually get his Tour victory in 1973, crushing the competition by a full fifteen minutes, but Merckx was not present. Ocaña also won the Vuelta in 1970, captured fifteen Grand Tour stages—nine in France and six in Spain—and won nine prestigious weeklong stage races between 1969 and 1973. The Spaniard's candle burned brightly, but only for a short time, as his Tour victory in 1973 would be his last big win; illness and crashes plagued him throughout the remainder of his career. Sadly, *Chepas* ("Humpy," as the peloton affectionately called him) took his own life at the age of forty-eight in in 1994, rather than suffer through the cancer he had kept hidden from the public.

RACE	POINTS	YEARS
THE MONUMENTS – 0 POINTS EARNED		
WORLD CHAMPIONSHIP ROAD RACE - I POINT EARNED		
BRONZE	I	1973
CLASSICS/OLYMPICS/TIME TRIALS – 2 POINTS EARNED		
GRAND PRIX DE NATIONS	2	1971
SEMI-CLASSICS/NATIONALS – 3 POINTS EARNED		
SPANISH NATIONAL RR CHAMPIONSHIPS	I	1968, 1972
TROFEO BARACCHI	I	1971

ADDITIONAL LUIS OCAÑA CONTINUED ON THE NEXT PAGE...

RACE	POINTS	YEARS
MINOR TOURS AND STAGE RACES – 25 POINTS EARNED		
VOLTA A CATALUNYA/TOUR OF CATALONIA	3	1971, 1973
TOUR OF THE BASQUE COUNTRY/VUELTA CICLISTA AL PAIS VASCO	3	1971, 1973
CRITÉRIUM DU DAUPHINÉ/CRITÉRIUM DU DAUPHINÉ LIBÉRÉ	3	1970, 1972, 1973
CATALAN WEEK/SETMANA CATALUNYA	2	1969
GP MIDI LIBRE	2	1969
GRAND TOURS (VARIOUS POINTS) - 19 POINTS EARNED		
TOUR DE FRANCE		
1ST PLACE	8	1973
VUELTA A ESPAÑA (TOUR OF SPAIN)		
1ST PLACE (PRE 1974)	4	1970
2ND PLACE	2	1969, 1973, 1976
3RD PLACE	1	1971
GRAND TOUR CLASSIFICATION JERSEYS – 2 POINTS EARNED		
VUELTA A ESPAÑA: MOUNTAINS	2	1969
GRAND TOUR STAGE WINS – 7.5 POINTS EARNED		
TOUR DE FRANCE: 9 STAGES	½ POINT	1970-1973
VUELTA A ESPAÑA: 6 STAGES	½ POINT	1969-1971
SEASON-LONG COMPETITIONS – 0 POINTS EARNED		
HOUR RECORD - 0 POINTS EARNED		
RACE RECORDS (VARIOUS POINTS) – 0 POINTS EARNED		
LIFETIME ACHIEVEMENTS (VARIOUS POINTS) – 0 POINTS EARNED		

Rank 35: Paolo Bettini

BORN: **APRIL 1, 1974**
YEARS ACTIVE: **1997–2008**
COUNTRY: **ITALY**
NICKNAME:
IL GRILLO (THE CRICKET)

CAREER WINS: **61**
TOTAL POINTS: **59**
RAW SCORE: **59**

BETTINI WAS ONE OF THE PREMIERE CLASSICS SPECIALISTS OF THE AUGHTS. He was not a man for the cobbles—after all, he was nicknamed "The Cricket"—but in any other terrain he was always a threat. He was great on the hills, had a tremendous sprint, and won a race in every single-day category, which also lead to winning three straight season-long competitions (UCI World Cup, 2002–2004); he also finished as the top-ranked rider in the 2003 UCI Road World Rankings. Bettini had a knack for winning the big ones, including Milan-San Remo in 2003, Liège in 2000 and 2002, Lombardia in 2005 and 2006, gold in the World Championship RR in 2006 and 2007, Zuri-Metzgete in 2001 and 2005, Clásica de San Sebastián in 2003, Italian RR Championships in 2003 and 2006, and gold in the Olympic Road Race in 2004. He was not a man for the high mountains, so the only category in which he didn't score points was in Grand Tours, but he did win two points classifications at the Giro in 2005 and 2006, and also won eight stages in all three GTs. *Il Grillo* also won Tirreno-Adriatico in 2004 and the Coppi e Bartali in 2000. That's quite the *palmarès*, given that Bettini had a relatively short eleven-year career.

RACE	POINTS	YEARS
THE MONUMENTS – 15 POINTS EARNED		
MILAN–SAN REMO:	3	2003
LIÈGE-BASTOGNE-LIÈGE	3	2000, 2002
IL LOMBARDIA/GIRO DI LOMBARDIA	3	2005, 2006
WORLD CHAMPIONSHIP ROAD RACE - 10 POINTS EARNED		
GOLD	4	2006, 2007
SILVER	2	2001
CLASSICS/OLYMPICS/TIME TRIALS – 8 POINTS EARNED		
OLYMPIC ROAD RACE GOLD	2	2004
CLÁSICA DE SAN SEBASTIÁN	2	2003
CHAMPIONSHIP OF ZURICH/ZÜRI-METZGETE	2	2001, 2005
SEMI-CLASSICS/NATIONALS – 5 POINTS EARNED		
ITALIAN NATIONAL RR CHAMPIONSHIPS	1	2003, 2006
GIRO DEL LAZIO	1	2002
EUROEYES CYCLASSICS/VATTENFALL CYCLASSICS, HEW CYCLASSICS	1	2003
COPPA PLACCI	1	2001
MINOR TOURS AND STAGE RACES – 5 POINTS EARNED		
TIRRENO–ADRIATICO	3	2004
SETTIMANA INTERNAZIONALE COPPI E BARTALI/GIRO DI SARDEGNA	2	2000
GRAND TOURS (VARIOUS POINTS) - 0 POINTS EARNED		

ADDITIONAL PAOLO BETTINI CONTINUED ON THE NEXT PAGE...

RACE	POINTS	YEARS
GRAND TOUR CLASSIFICATION JERSEYS – 4 POINTS EARNED		
GIRO D'ITALIA: POINTS	2	2005, 2006
GRAND TOUR STAGE WINS – 4 POINTS EARNED		
GIRO D'ITALIA: 2 STAGES	½ POINT	2005-2006
TOUR DE FRANCE: 1 STAGE	½ POINT	2000
VUELTA A ESPAÑA: 5 STAGES	½ POINT	2005-2011
SEASON-LONG COMPETITIONS – 8 POINTS EARNED		
UCI ROAD WORLD CUP	2	2002, 2003, 2004
UCI ROAD WORLD ROAD RANKINGS	2	2003
HOUR RECORD - 0 POINTS EARNED		
RACE RECORDS (VARIOUS POINTS) – 0 POINTS EARNED		
LIFETIME ACHIEVEMENTS (VARIOUS POINTS) – 0 POINTS EARNED		

Rank 36: Fabian Cancellara

BORN: **MARCH 18, 1981**
YEARS ACTIVE: **2001–2016**
COUNTRY: **SWITZERLAND**
NICKNAME: **SPARTACUS**

CAREER WINS: **87**
TOTAL POINTS: **59**
RAW SCORE: **56**

ALONG WITH TOM BOONEN, CANCELLARA WAS THE PREMIER cobbled Classics champion of his era, capturing three victories in both Flanders and Paris-Roubaix. It should come as no surprise that he also won E3 Harelbeke three times. "Sparticus" would also claim *La Primavera*, Milan-San Remo, in 2008. As a testament to his incredible consistency, Cancellara finished on the podium a whopping sixteen times in the first three Monuments of the season, Milan-San Remo, Flanders, and Paris-Roubaix. He was also a brilliant time trialist and was the world champion in the discipline four times, in addition to being the gold medalist in the race against the clock in both the 2008 and 2016 Summer Olympics. Although no points are earned in this scoring system, he also won his national time trial championship ten times. Cancellara had great success capturing the opening prologue of Tour de France, and would often wear the yellow jersey for extended periods of time during the early parts of the race; he holds the distinction of wearing the jersey for twenty-nine days, which is the most of any cyclist who hasn't actually won the event.

RACE	POINTS	YEARS
THE MONUMENTS – 24 POINTS EARNED		
MILAN–SAN REMO:	3	2008
TOUR OF FLANDERS/RONDE VAN VLAANDEREN	3	2010, 2013, 2014
PARIS–ROUBAIX	4	2006, 2010, 2013
WORLD CHAMPIONSHIP ROAD RACE - 0 POINTS EARNED		
CLASSICS/OLYMPICS/TIME TRIALS – 12 POINTS EARNED		
OLYMPIC TT GOLD	2	2008, 2016
WORLD TT GOLD	2	2006, 2007, 2009, 2010
SEMI-CLASSICS/NATIONALS – 5 POINTS EARNED		
SWISS NATIONAL RR CHAMPIONSHIPS	I	2009, 2011
E3 BINKBANK CLASSIC/E3 HARELBEKE/ HARELBEKE–ANTWERP–HARELBEKE/E3 PRIJS VLAANDEREN	I	2010, 2011, 2013
MINOR TOURS AND STAGE RACES – 9 POINTS EARNED		
TIRRENO–ADRIATICO	3	2008, 2015,
TOUR OF SWITZERLAND/TOUR DE SUISSE	3	2009
GRAND TOURS (VARIOUS POINTS) - 0 POINTS EARNED		
GRAND TOUR CLASSIFICATION JERSEYS – 0 POINTS EARNED		
GRAND TOUR STAGE WINS - 6 POINTS EARNED		
TOUR DE FRANCE: 8 STAGES	½ POINT	2004-2012
VUELTA A ESPAÑA: 3 STAGES, 1 TTT	½ POINT	2009-2013
SEASON-LONG COMPETITIONS – 0 POINTS EARNED		
HOUR RECORD – 0 POINTS EARNED		
RACE RECORDS (VARIOUS POINTS) – 3 POINTS EARNED		
TOUR OF FLANDERS: 3 POINTS (SHARED WITH ACHIEL BUYSSE, FIORENZO MAGNI, ERIC LEMAN, JOHAN MUSEEUW, AND TOM BOONEN)		
LIFETIME ACHIEVEMENTS (VARIOUS POINTS) – 0 POINTS EARNED		

Rank 37: Charly Gaul

BORN: **DECEMBER 8, 1932**
YEARS ACTIVE: **1953–1965**
COUNTRY: **LUXEMBOURG**
NICKNAME:
LA ANGLE DE MONTAGNE
(ANGEL OF THE MOUNTAINS)

CAREER WINS: **48**
TOTAL POINTS: **57.5**
RAW SCORE: **57.5**

GAUL IS LUXEMBOURG'S TOP-RANKED CYCLIST, another one of the legendary climbers from the golden age of cycling's postwar era, reaching the heights of his success in the mid to late 1950s. The "Angel of the Mountains" won the Tour de France in 1958 and the Giro d'Italia twice, in 1956 and 1959. Each of those victories was punctuated by a miraculous come-from-behind victory, two of them in atrociously cold weather conditions.

At the start of the eighteenth stage in the 1956 Giro, Gaul was lying in twenty-fourth place, over sixteen minutes behind the leader, Pasquale Fornara. At the foot of the last climb, Monte Bondone, with 88 kilometers (58 miles) yet to race, it started to snow. The snow became a blizzard, and rider after rider, including the race leader, was forced to take shelter from the cold. Not Gaul. He flew up the mountain, rapidly spinning the low gears that were a trademark of his pedaling style. By the end of the stage, eighty cyclists had abandoned the race, and Gaul would don the pink jersey with a buffer of 3 minutes, 27 seconds over Fiorenzo Magni. He maintained this margin over the next two stages, taking his first victory in a Grand Tour. He basically won the race with one perfectly timed attack.

Like his first Giro victory, a similar scenario played out in the 1958 Tour de France. Gaul had set the record climbing Mont Ventoux during the stage eighteen uphill time trial (a mark that wouldn't be broken for thirty-one years), but by the end of the twentieth stage he'd found himself back in sixth place, over sixteen minutes off the lead, primarily due to a mechanical breakdown suffered during the mountainous stage nineteen. The twenty-first stage was another epic alpine stage that included five mountains, and once again mother nature intervened to deal Charly Gaul another winning hand—a storm front moved in, and with it, torrential rain, plummeting temperatures, and wind. As the downpour started on the second climb of the day, the Angel of the Mountains took flight once again, leaving all others in his wake. On the descent, then race leader Rafaël Géminiani had some amazing talent to help him try and close gap to the Luxembourger: Louison Bobet, Jacques Anquetil, and Federico Bahamontes. Unbelievably, these three legends continued to lose time to Gaul. Although he didn't take the yellow jersey by the end of the stage, Gaul gained over fifteen minutes on Géminiani and found himself only 1 minute, 7 seconds down, in third place. Gaul was also a gifted time trialist—in the penultimate 75 kilometer stage twenty-three individual time trial, he put over three minutes into both Géminiani and the current race leader, Vito Favero. Gaul won the forty-fifth Tour de France with another legendary performance in horrible weather.

He'd repeat his come-from-behind heroics in the 1959 Giro, but without the aid of inclement weather. This time Gaul found himself in second place, 3 minutes, 36 seconds adrift of none other than Jacques Anquetil, with only the penultimate mountainous stage

ADDITIONAL CHARLY GAUL CONTINUED ON THE NEXT PAGE...

twenty-one left. Anquetil forgot to eat properly during that stage and completely blew up, ceding almost ten minutes. Gaul won that Giro by 6 minutes, 12 seconds, once again securing victory in a Grand Tour with one death blow delivered to his rivals in a mountain stage. That Giro triumph would prove to be his last GT victory. As befitting *La Angle de Montagne*, he also claimed the mountains classification in the 1955 and 1956 Tour, and in both of his Giro wins in 1956 and 1959. His *palmarès* would include twenty-one Grand Tour stage victories, ten in the Tour and eleven in the Giro. He is certainly one of the candidates for the title of best pure climber in the sport's history.

RACE	POINTS	YEARS
THE MONUMENTS – 0 POINTS EARNED		
WORLD CHAMPIONSHIP ROAD RACE - 1 POINT EARNED		
BRONZE	1	1954
CLASSICS/OLYMPICS/TIME TRIALS – 0 POINTS EARNED		
SEMI-CLASSICS/NATIONALS – 6 POINTS EARNED		
LUXEMBOURG NATIONAL RR CHAMPIONSHIPS	1	1956, 1957, 1959, 1960, 1961, 1962
MINOR TOURS AND STAGE RACES – 6 POINTS EARNED		
TOUR DE LUXEMBOURG	2	1956, 1959, 1961
GRAND TOURS (VARIOUS POINTS) - 26 POINTS EARNED		
GIRO D'ITALIA		
1ST PLACE	6	1956, 1959
3RD PLACE	1	1958, 1960
TOUR DE FRANCE		
1ST PLACE	8	1958
3RD PLACE	2	1955, 1961
RACE	POINTS	YEARS
GRAND TOUR CLASSIFICATION JERSEYS – 8 POINTS EARNED		
GIRO D'ITALIA: MOUNTAINS	2	1956, 1959
TOUR DE FRANCE: MOUNTAINS	2	1955, 1956
GRAND TOUR STAGE WINS – 10.5 POINTS EARNED		
GIRO D'ITALIA: 11 STAGES	½ POINT	1956-1962
TOUR DE FRANCE: 10 STAGES	½ POINT	1953-1963
SEASON-LONG COMPETITIONS – 0 POINTS EARNED		
HOUR RECORD - 0 POINTS EARNED		
RACE RECORDS (VARIOUS POINTS) – 0 POINTS EARNED		
LIFETIME ACHIEVEMENTS (VARIOUS POINTS) – 0 POINTS EARNED		

Rank 38: Franco Bitossi

BORN: **SEPTEMBER 1, 1940**
YEARS ACTIVE: **1961–1978**
COUNTRY: **ITALY**
NICKNAME:
CUORE MATTO (CRAZY HEART)

CAREER WINS: **98**
TOTAL POINTS: **57**
RAW SCORE: **57**

ANOTHER ONE OF THOSE INTRIGUING "WHAT IF" SCENARIOS. Bitossi had a cardiac arrhythmia, thus earning him the nickname *Cuore Matto* (or "Crazy Heart"), which sometimes required him to stop in the middle of a race, especially early in his career. What if he hadn't had such a condition? How much more might he have won? Bitossi had a long career, turning pro as soon as he was able at the age of twenty-one in October 1961, and he was still competitive late into his career, winning the Italian RR Championship in 1976 and a bronze medal in the 1977 World Championship RR, one year before he retired. He was never really a favorite for any of the Grand Tours, but he was a gifted climber and an accomplished single-day racer. He won the points classification in the Tour in 1968 and the Giro in 1969 and 1970, also capturing the mountains classification in the Giro three years in a row (1964–1966). His career *palmarès* included twenty-four Grand Tour stages, the Giro di Lombardia (1967 and 1970), Italian National RR Championships (1970 and 1976), Zuri-Metzgete (1965 and 1968), and numerous victories in a variety of Italian Semi-Classics. Although he didn't land on the podium in any

Grand Tours, he did have success in weeklong Minor Tours, claiming the 1965 Tour of Switzerland, the 1967 Tirenno-Adriatico, and the 1970 Volta a Catalunya.

Bitossi had quite a distinguished career, but one of his most memorable races unfortunately ended up as a near miss, with victory snatched away at the line by a teammate in the 1972 World Championship Road Race. In the closing kilometers, Bitossi went off the front of the vastly reduced peloton, a small group that included such luminaries as Eddy Merckx, Cyrille Guimard, Joop Zoetemelk, Michele Dancelli, Leif Mortensen, Frans Verbeeck, and fellow Italian Marino Basso. As the line approached, and with the group rapidly closing in, Bitossi found that he was slightly overgeared and changed his line to the middle of the road. Away from the shelter provided by the crowds at the side of the road, he caught a cross-headwind. He took one look back as the line approached but never saw that the group was bearing down on him, led by none other than Basso. There was a race vehicle blocking his view, and he was passed just meters before the line. It was an epic win for Basso, but it came at the expense of poor Crazy Heart, his own teammate whom he'd chased down. Bitossi placed second in that race, so he certainly would have held off the rest of the group had it not been for Basso.

ADDITIONAL FRANCO BITOSSI CONTINUED ON THE NEXT PAGE...

RACE	POINTS	YEARS
THE MONUMENTS - 6 POINTS EARNED		
IL LOMBARDIA/GIRO DI LOMBARDIA	3	1967, 1970
WORLD CHAMPIONSHIP ROAD RACE - 3 POINTS EARNED		
SILVER	2	1972, 1977
CLASSICS/OLYMPICS/TIME TRIALS - 4 POINTS EARNED		
CHAMPIONSHIP OF ZURICH/ZURI-METZGETE	2	1965, 1968
SEMI-CLASSICS/NATIONALS - 11 POINTS EARNED		
ITALIAN NATIONAL RR CHAMPIONSHIPS	1	1970, 1971, 1976
GIRO DI LAZIO	1	1965
GIRO DELLA ROMAGNA	1	1971, 1974
GIRO DELLA TOSCANA	1	1968
MILANO-TORINO/MILAN-TURIN	1	1968
GIRO DELL'EMILIA	1	1970, 1973
GIRO DEL VENETO	1	1970 (SERVED AS NATIONAL CHAMPION-SHIP), 1973

RACE	POINTS	YEARS
MINOR TOURS AND STAGE RACES – 9 POINTS EARNED		
TIRRENO–ADRIATICO	3	1967
VOLTA A CATALUNYA/TOUR OF CATALONIA	3	1970
TOUR OF SWITZERLAND/TOUR DE SUISSE	3	1965
GRAND TOURS (VARIOUS POINTS) - 0 POINTS EARNED		
GRAND TOUR CLASSIFICATION JERSEYS – 12 POINTS EARNED		
GIRO D'ITALIA: POINTS	2	1969, 1970
TOUR DE FRANCE: POINTS	2	1968
GIRO D'ITALIA: MOUNTAINS	2	1964, 1965, 1966
GRAND TOUR STAGE WINS - 12 POINTS EARNED		
GIRO D'ITALIA: 20 STAGES	½ POINT	1964–1975
TOUR DE FRANCE: 4 STAGES	½ POINT	1966–1968
SEASON-LONG COMPETITIONS – 0 POINTS EARNED		
HOUR RECORD - 0 POINTS EARNED		
RACE RECORDS (VARIOUS POINTS) – 0 POINTS EARNED		
LIFETIME ACHIEVEMENTS (VARIOUS POINTS) – 0 POINTS EARNED		

Rank 39: Mark Cavendish

BORN: **MAY 21, 1985**
YEARS ACTIVE: **2005–PRESENT**
COUNTRY: **BRITAIN**
NICKNAME: **THE MANX MISSILE**

CAREER WINS: **149**
TOTAL POINTS: **56.5**
RAW SCORE: **46.5**

As I WRITE THIS IN LATE 2019, "The Manx Missile's" prior three seasons have been rough. Illness and crashes have contributed to exactly one win in 2017, another single victory in 2018, and no wins in the 2019 season. After Merckx, he has the most Tour de France stage victories—thirty—and is only five away from breaking the record, yet he hasn't won a stage in that race since 2016; his team didn't even select him to participate in the 2019 edition. With 149 victories, Cavendish is only a single win short of getting a ten-point bonus and joining only seven other cyclists who have achieved 150 road victories over the course of their career; he'd jump up at least ten places in the rankings. At this point, it's rather unlikely that he'll overtake Mario Cipollini to become known as the sport's greatest pure sprinter. I'm hoping that the Manx Missile can get back to full power and health, but I'm also wondering if the many bad crashes he's had in recent years have simply taken too great of a toll on his body. Cavendish has switched to a new a new team for the 2020 season; maybe the change will be just the thing needed to help him find his way back to the top step of the podium.

RACE	POINTS	YEARS
THE MONUMENTS – 3 POINTS EARNED		
MILAN–SAN REMO:	3	2009
WORLD CHAMPIONSHIP ROAD RACE - 6 POINTS EARNED		
GOLD	4	2014
SILVER	2	2016
CLASSICS/OLYMPICS/TIME TRIALS – 0 POINTS EARNED		
SEMI-CLASSICS/NATIONALS – 6 POINTS EARNED		
BRITISH NATIONAL RR CHAMPIONSHIPS	I	2013
KUURNE–BRUSSELS–KUURNE	I	2012, 2105
SCHELDEPRIJS/GP DE L'ESCAUT/GROTE SCHELDEPRIJS/ SCHELDEPRIJS VLAANDEREN	I	2007, 2008, 2011
MINOR TOURS AND STAGE RACES – 0 POINTS EARNED		
GRAND TOURS (VARIOUS POINTS) - 0 POINTS EARNED		
GRAND TOUR CLASSIFICATION JERSEYS – 6 POINTS EARNED		
GIRO D'ITALIA: POINTS	2	2013
TOUR DE FRANCE: POINTS	2	2011
VUELTA A ESPAÑA: POINTS	2	2010
GRAND TOUR STAGE WINS – 25.5 POINTS EARNED		
GIRO D'ITALIA: 15 STAGES, 2 TTT	½ POINT	2008-2013
TOUR DE FRANCE: 30 STAGES	½ POINT	2008-2016
VUELTA A ESPAÑA: 3 STAGES, I TTT	½ POINT	2010
SEASON-LONG COMPETITIONS – 0 POINTS EARNED		
HOUR RECORD - 0 POINTS EARNED		
RACE RECORDS (VARIOUS POINTS) – 0 POINTS EARNED		
LIFETIME ACHIEVEMENTS (VARIOUS POINTS) – IO POINTS EARNED		
WON 30 GRAND TOUR STAGES: IO PTS		

Rank 40: Gianni Bugno

BORN: **FEBRUARY 14, 1964**
YEARS ACTIVE: **1985-1998**
COUNTRY: **ITALY**
NICKNAME: **THE LIZARD**

CAREER WINS: **59**
TOTAL POINTS: **54.5**
RAW SCORE: **54.5**

BUGNO COULD SPRINT WELL AND WAS AN EXCELLENT CLIMBER, a highly capable time trialist, and comfortable on the cobbles. It was a rare skill set, reminiscent of some of the best all-rounders in the sport, but his flame burned brightly for but a brief period of time in the early 1990s. He turned pro in 1986 and won some of the Italian Semi-Classics in his first three seasons. He also won a stage in the 1988 Tour and 1989 Giro, but these results were not exactly a harbinger of what was to come over the next few years.

Bugno's 1990 season started in spectacular fashion with victory in Milan-San Remo. His next win came in the Giro d'Italia tune-up stage race, the Giro del Trentino. Bugno was obviously in great shape, but nobody could have guessed that he would go on to dominate the Giro d'Italia, leading the race from start to finish, collecting both time trial stages, a mountain stage, and the points classification. Only Costante Girardengo, Alfredo Binda, and Eddy Merckx had ever worn the pink jersey from the beginning of the race to the end. It was the stuff of legends, but Bugno never again matched the dominance of that Giro victory. Following that huge win, he raced the Tour de France, finishing seventh overall and winning two stages. One of those stage wins featured the finishing climb up the iconic Alpe d'Huez, with Bugno narrowly defeating eventual race winner Greg LeMond by a bike throw at the line. His amazing year was capped by winning the season-long competition, at the time the UCI World Cup, also finishing atop the year-end UCI World Ranking.

Bugno had a quiet start to the 1991 season. Still favored to win the Giro that year, he faded in a couple of the mountain stages and finished off the podium in fourth place, yet he still managed to collect three stage wins. He then won the Italian National RR Championship and headed to the Tour de France, finishing a respectable second place, 3 minutes, 36 seconds behind Miguel Indurain—his first of five straight victories. Bugno followed this up by winning the Clásica de San Sebastián. He then exacted his revenge on Indurain in the World Championship RR by defeating him and Steven Rooks in the sprint to the line. It was another spectacular year, and Bugno again finished at the top of the list in the UCI World Ranking.

In his 1992 season, Bugno finished third in the Tour, but without any stage wins. He once again rose to the occasion and won the sprint finish in the World Championship RR, this time pipping Laurent Jalabert and Dmitri Konyshev (Rooks and Indurain, the previous year's silver and bronze medalists, were also beat in that sprint). The season again ended on a high note, with three more victories in Italy's prestigious Semi-Classics, Milan-Turin, the Giro di Lazio, and the Giro dell'Emilia. His only 1993 victory in this scoring system would be the Grand Prix Gippingen. Just when it looked like his star was about to fade, Bugno pulled off a shocker in 1994 by defeating none other than Johan Museeuw in one of his favorite playgrounds, the Tour of Flanders. Although Bugno did win the 1995 National RR Championship and two more stages in both the Giro and Vuelta,

ADDITIONAL GIANNI BUGNO CONTINUED ON THE NEXT PAGE...

that Flanders victory in '94 would prove to be his last big win; his last three years played out remarkably like his first three, with little fanfare. In fact, his last victories were spaced two years apart—a stage win in the 1996 Vuelta and then his last in 1998, also a stage in Spain's Grand Tour. His rapid rise and fall would be mirrored by another of his contemporaries in the Top 50, Claudio Chiappucci.

RACE	POINTS	YEARS
THE MONUMENTS – 6 POINTS EARNED		
MILAN–SAN REMO:	3	1990
TOUR OF FLANDERS/RONDE VAN VLAANDEREN	3	1994
WORLD CHAMPIONSHIP ROAD RACE - 9 POINTS EARNED		
GOLD	4	1991, 1992
BRONZE	1	1990
CLASSICS/OLYMPICS/TIME TRIALS – 2 POINTS EARNED		
CLÁSICA DE SAN SEBASTIÁN	2	1991
SEMI-CLASSICS/NATIONALS – 8 POINTS EARNED		
ITALIAN NATIONAL RR CHAMPIONSHIPS	1	1991, 1995
GIRO DEL LAZIO/ROMA MAXIMA	1	1992
GRAND PRIX OF AARGAU CANTON/GP GIPPENGEN	1	1993
MILANO–TORINO/MILAN–TURIN	1	1992
GIRO DELL'EMILIA	1	1992
TRE VALLE VARESINE	1	1989
GRAN PIEMONTE/GIRO DEL PIEMONTE	1	1986

RACE	POINTS	YEARS
MINOR TOURS AND STAGE RACES – 2 POINTS EARNED		
TOUR OF THE ALPS/GIRO DEL TRENTINO	2	1990
GRAND TOURS (VARIOUS POINTS) - 12 POINTS EARNED		
GIRO D'ITALIA		
1ST PLACE	6	1990
TOUR DE FRANCE		
2ND PLACE	4	1991
3RD PLACE	2	1992
GRAND TOUR CLASSIFICATION JERSEYS – 2 POINTS EARNED		
GIRO D'ITALIA: POINTS	2	1990
GRAND TOUR STAGE WINS – 7.5 POINTS EARNED		
GIRO D'ITALIA: 9 STAGES	½ POINT	1989-1996
TOUR DE FRANCE: 4 STAGES	½ POINT	1988-1991
VUELTA A ESPAÑA: 2 STAGES	½ POINT	1996-1998
SEASON-LONG COMPETITIONS – 6 POINTS EARNED		
UCI ROAD WORLD CUP	2	1990
UCI ROAD WORLD ROAD RANKINGS	2	1990, 1991
HOUR RECORD - 0 POINTS EARNED		
RACE RECORDS (VARIOUS POINTS) - 0 POINTS EARNED		
LIFETIME ACHIEVEMENTS (VARIOUS POINTS) - 0 POINTS EARNED		

Rank 41: Philippe Gilbert

BORN: **JULY 5, 1982**
YEARS ACTIVE: **2003 - PRESENT**
COUNTRY: **BELGIUM**
NICKNAME: **BOAR OF THE ARDENNES**

CAREER WINS: **77**
TOTAL POINTS: **52.5**
RAW SCORE: **52.5**

GILBERT IS A SINGLE-DAY SPECIALIST BEST KNOWN for being only
the second cyclist to capture all three of the Ardennes Classics
in a single year– the Amstel Gold, La Flèche Wallone, and Liège-
Bastogne-Liège. "The Boar of the Ardennes" accomplished this
in 2011, and he shares this honor with Davide Rebellin, the first
to manage this rare treble of victories in 2004. Gilbert is the only
cyclist to have also won the Ardennes Semi-Classic, Brabanse Pijl,
in the same year as the other three Classics, thus becoming the sole
owner of the Ardennes "quadruple." He won 18 races in 2011, the
most of any in the peloton; these included the Belgian RR and TT
championship, the Tour of Belgium, the Clásica de San Sebastián, a
stage of the Tour de France, and as no surprise, the UCI World Tour
title.

Gilbert's knack for stringing together big victories was first realized
in 2009 when over a ten-day period he won the Coppa Sabatini, Giro
del Piemonte, Paris-Tours, and the Giro di Lombardia, closing out
the season with a bang. In 2017 he became only the third rider, after

Eddy Merckx and Jan Raas, to have won Flanders and Amstel Gold in the same year. In 2019, after capturing Paris-Roubaix, Gilbert joined Louison Bobet, Germain Derycke, Alfred De Bruyne, Sean Kelly, and Hennie Kuiper as winners of four of the five different Monuments. Should he capture that one missing Monument from his *palmarès*, Milan-San Remo, he will join only Rik Van Looy, Merckx, and Roger De Vlaeminck as the only other cyclists to win all five of the Monuments and pick up a huge 15-point bonus. It is interesting that Milan-San Remo is the one needed to complete the feat, as he's come very close already by placing third in both 2008 and 2011, losing both in the reduced bunch sprint for the line.

The other significant victory by the Belgian was his gold medal in the 2012 World Championship RR. Such are the breadth of his wins that Gilbert is now only two victories away from landing a 10-point bonus for capturing 25 wins in all single-day races. In August of 2019 The Boar of the Ardennes signed a three-year deal with the Lotto Soudal team; it's entirely possible that if he has another one of his legendary winning streaks over the next few years, he may end up in the Top 25 by the end of his career.

RACE	POINTS	YEARS
THE MONUMENTS – 16 POINTS EARNED		
TOUR OF FLANDERS/RONDE VAN VLAANDEREN	3	2017
PARIS-ROUBAIX	4	2019
LIÈGE-BASTOGNE-LIÈGE	3	2011
IL LOMBARDIA/GIRO DI LOMBARDIA	3	2009, 2010
WORLD CHAMPIONSHIP ROAD RACE – 4 POINTS EARNED		
GOLD	4	2012

ADDITIONAL PHILIPPE GILBERT CONTINUED ON THE NEXT PAGE...

RACE	POINTS	YEARS
CLASSICS/OLYMPICS/TIME TRIALS – 14 POINTS EARNED		
AMSTEL GOLD	2	2010, 2011, 2014, 2017
LA FLÈCHE WALLONNE	2	2011
CLÁSICA DE SAN SEBASTIÁN	2	2011
PARIS–TOURS	2	2008, 2009
SEMI-CLASSICS/NATIONALS – 9 POINTS EARNED		
BELGIAN NATIONAL CHAMPIONSHIPS	1	2011, 2016
OMLOOP HET NIEUWSBLAD/HET VOLK	1	2006, 2008
BRABANTSE PIJL/FLÈCHE BRABANÇONNE	1	2011, 2014
GRAND PRIX DE FOURMIES	1	2006
GRAN PIEMONTE/GIRO DEL PIEMONTE	1	2009, 2010
MINOR TOURS AND STAGE RACES – 2 POINTS EARNED		
TOUR OF BELGIUM	2	2011
GRAND TOURS (VARIOUS POINTS) - 0 POINTS EARNED		
GRAND TOUR CLASSIFICATION JERSEYS – 0 POINTS EARNED		
GRAND TOUR STAGE WINS – 5.5 POINTS EARNED		
GIRO D'ITALIA: 1 STAGE	½ POINT	2011
TOUR DE FRANCE: 3 STAGES	½ POINT	2009-2015
VUELTA A ESPAÑA: 7 STAGES	½ POINT	2010-2019
SEASON-LONG COMPETITIONS – 2 POINTS EARNED		
UCI WORLD TOUR ('09-PRESENT)	2	2011
HOUR RECORD - 0 POINTS EARNED		
RACE RECORDS (VARIOUS POINTS) – 0 POINTS EARNED		
LIFETIME ACHIEVEMENTS (VARIOUS POINTS) – 0 POINTS EARNED		

Rank 42: Jan Raas

BORN: **NOVEMBER 8, 1952**
YEARS ACTIVE: **1975–1985**
COUNTRY: **NETHERLANDS**
NICKNAME: **AMSTEL GOLD RAAS**

CAREER WINS: **68**
TOTAL POINTS: **51.5**
RAW SCORE: **51.5**

RAAS WAS A PROLIFIC SPRING CLASSICS SPECIALIST WINNER FROM THE
LATE 1970S AND EARLY 1980S. He had a gift for reading races and was
a great sprinter. Raas didn't always need to rely on outkicking others
to the line; he often powered off the front of a surviving group of lead
riders late into a race, distancing himself from anyone who attempted
to follow his wheel. He wasn't a man for long climbs or mountains,
but his devastating power was used to full effect in the shorter
steep hills found in many of the northern spring Classics. Raas is
best remembered as the cyclist who practically owned the Amstel
Gold race, winning five of the six editions he entered from 1977
to 1980 and 1982 and earning the nickname "Amstel Gold Raas."
The highlights of his career include a victory in the 1977 Milan-San
Remo, two Tour of Flanders wins in 1979 and 1983, Paris-Roubaix in
1982, a gold in the 1979 World Championship RR, Ghent-Wevelgem
in 1981, Paris-Tours in both 1978 and 1981, seven Belgian Semi-
Classics, three Belgian National RR Championships, the Tour of
Holland in 1979, and ten stages in the Tour de France. Raas was only
one victory shy of winning twenty-five single-day races in this scoring
system; had he done so, he'd have finished about ten places higher,
which is pretty remarkable given he had a fairly short 10-year career.

RACE	POINTS	YEARS
THE MONUMENTS – 13 POINTS EARNED		
MILAN–SAN REMO:	3	1977
TOUR OF FLANDERS/RONDE VAN VLAANDEREN	3	1979, 1983
PARIS–ROUBAIX	4	1982
WORLD CHAMPIONSHIP ROAD RACE - 4 POINTS EARNED		
GOLD	4	1979
CLASSICS/OLYMPICS/TIME TRIALS – 16 POINTS EARNED		
GHENT–WEVELGEM	2	1981
AMSTEL GOLD	2	1977, 1978, 1979, 1980, 1982
PARIS–TOURS	2	1978, 1981
SEMI-CLASSICS/NATIONALS – 11 POINTS EARNED		
NETHERLANDS NATIONAL RR CHAMPIONSHIPS	1	1976, 1983, 1984
OMLOOP HET NIEUWSBLAD/HET VOLK	1	1981
KUURNE–BRUSSELS–KUURNE	1	1980, 1983
DWARS DOOR VLAANDEREN	1	1982
E3 BINKBANK CLASSIC/E3 HARELBEKE/HARELBEKE–ANT-WERP–HARELBEKE/E3 PRIJS VLAANDEREN	1	1979, 1980, 1981
BRUSSELS CYCLING CLASSIC/PARIS–BRUSSELS (POST 1966 EDITIONS)	1	1978
MINOR TOURS AND STAGE RACES – 2 POINTS EARNED		
BINCKBANK TOUR/ENECO TOUR OF BENELUX/RONDE VAN NEDERLANDS	2	1979
GRAND TOURS (VARIOUS POINTS) - 0 POINTS EARNED		
GRAND TOUR CLASSIFICATION JERSEYS – 0 POINTS EARNED		
GRAND TOUR STAGE WINS - 5.5 POINTS EARNED		
TOUR DE FRANCE: 10 STAGES, 1 TTT	½ POINT	1977–1984
SEASON-LONG COMPETITIONS – 0 POINTS EARNED		
HOUR RECORD - 0 POINTS EARNED		
RACE RECORDS (VARIOUS POINTS) – 0 POINTS EARNED		
LIFETIME ACHIEVEMENTS (VARIOUS POINTS) – 0 POINTS EARNED		

Rank 43: Moreno Argentin

BORN: **DECEMBER 17, 1960**
YEARS ACTIVE: **1980-1994**
COUNTRY: **ITALY**
NICKNAME:
IL CAPO (THE BOSS)

CAREER WINS: **69**
TOTAL POINTS: **51**
RAW SCORE: **51**

ARGENTIN WAS ONE OF THE GREAT CLASSICS SPECIALISTS FROM THE
1980S AND EARLY 1990S. The Italian possessed a wicked sprint and
would often victimize anyone trying to hold his wheel on the steep
climbs. He was most brilliant in the Ardennes Classics, winning the
La Flèche Wallone in 1990, 1991, and 1994, and more significantly,
three straight Liège-Bastogne-Liège victories from 1985 to 1987,
and again in 1991. It's not surprising that a cyclist with his talents
was also world champion on the hilly course in Colorado Springs
in 1986, or that he won the Giro di Lombardia in 1987, but as a
testament to his strength and versatility, "The Boss" was also able
to claim victory in the 1990 Tour of Flanders. Not a slight climber
built for the high mountains, Argentin did reach the third step of
the podium in the 1984 Giro, finishing behind Francesco Moser and
Laurent Fignon. His *palmarès* included thirteen stage wins in the
Italian GT, as well as two in the Tour de France. Despite all those
significant wins, he's also well remembered for a stinging loss—
the 1992 Milan-San Remo. Argentin had gapped the field by eight

seconds over the finishing Poggio climb, but Sean Kelly was in hot pursuit, bombing down the switchbacks on a kamikaze-like mission to catch up to the Italian. "King Kelly" latched onto the Italian's back wheel at the bottom of the descent with only about a kilometer left in the race. With the rest of peloton barreling down on them as they played a bit of cat and mouse, Kelly outsprinted Argentin in the closing meters, winning one of the most memorable Milan-San Remo editions in history.

RACE	POINTS	YEARS
THE MONUMENTS – 18 POINTS EARNED		
TOUR OF FLANDERS/RONDE VAN VLAANDEREN	3	1990
LIÈGE-BASTOGNE-LIÈGE	3	1985, 1986, 1987, 1991
IL LOMBARDIA/GIRO DI LOMBARDIA	3	1987
WORLD CHAMPIONSHIP ROAD RACE – 7 POINTS EARNED		
GOLD	4	1986
SILVER	2	1987
BRONZE	1	1985
CLASSICS/OLYMPICS/TIME TRIALS – 6 POINTS EARNED		
LA FLÈCHE WALLONNE	2	1990, 1991, 1994
SEMI-CLASSICS/NATIONALS – 4 POINTS EARNED		
ITALIAN NATIONAL RR CHAMPIONSHIPS	1	1983, 1989
GIRO DELLA ROMAGNA	1	1982
GIRO DEL VENETO	1	1984, 1988

ADDITIONAL MORENO ARGENTIN CONTINUED ON THE NEXT PAGE...

RACE	POINTS	YEARS
MINOR TOURS AND STAGE RACES – 6 POINTS EARNED		
SETTIMANA INTERNAZIONALE COPPI E BARTALI/GIRO DI SARDEGNA	2	1984, 1992
TOUR OF THE ALPS/GIRO DEL TRENTINO	2	1994
GRAND TOURS (VARIOUS POINTS) - 1 POINT EARNED		
GIRO D'ITALIA		
3RD PLACE	1	1984
GRAND TOUR CLASSIFICATION JERSEYS – 0 POINTS EARNED		
GRAND TOUR STAGE WINS - 8 POINTS EARNED		
GIRO D'ITALIA: 13 STAGES	½ POINT	1981-1984
TOUR DE FRANCE: 2 STAGES, 1 TTT	½ POINT	1987-1993
SEASON-LONG COMPETITIONS – 0 POINTS EARNED		
HOUR RECORD - 0 POINTS EARNED		
RACE RECORDS (VARIOUS POINTS) – 0 POINTS EARNED		
LIFETIME ACHIEVEMENTS (VARIOUS POINTS) – 0 POINTS EARNED		

Rank 44: Claudio Chiappucci

BORN: **FEBRUARY 28, 1963**
YEARS ACTIVE: **1985-1998**
COUNTRY: **ITALY**
NICKNAME: *EL DIABLO* (THE DEVIL)

CAREER WINS: **33**
TOTAL POINTS: **50.5**
RAW SCORE: **50.5**

EL DIABLO'S CAREER IS STRANGELY SIMILAR TO THAT OF GIANNI
BUGNO. Both turned pro in the mid-1980s, experienced fairly limited
success their first few years, then burst on the scene in 1990 with
surprising Grand Tour success. Each of them had a remarkable
three-year run in the early 1990s, and then both of them faded away
in the final few years of their careers. Chiappucci announced himself
to the cycling world by capturing the mountains classification in the
1990 Giro. His next breakthrough came in that July's Tour de France,
when he found himself in a four-man breakaway that finished ten
minutes ahead of the peloton. The Italian clung tenaciously to his
lead through the mountains, finally succumbing to Greg LeMond in
the penultimate stage twenty time trial. Chiappucci would finish on
the second step of the podium, 2 minutes, 16 seconds in arrears. The
time trial would prove to be his Grand Tour Achilles heel, and would
prevent him from ever claiming first place. He did have great success
in GTs, finishing second in France in 1990 and 1992, and third in
1991. He was also second in the Giro in 1991 and 1992, and third in
1993. A gifted climber, he would claim the mountains competition

in five Grand Tours—the Tour in 1991 and 1992, and the Giro in 1990, 1992, and 1993. Chiappucci also won the points classification in the 1991 Tour and captured four GT stages, one in Italy and three in France. His successes were not merely limited to Grand Tours—he won the Tour of the Basque Country in 1991, the Giro del Trentino in 1992, and the Volta a Catalunya in 1994. Chiappucci's single-day victories included four of the Italian Semi-Classics, the 1993 Clásica de San Sebastián, and most significantly, his single Monument victory in the 1991 Milan-San Remo. He retired in 1998, but his last victory in this point scoring system would the Gran Piemonte in 1995. His last three years were just as quiet as his first four years as a professional, but were devoid of even a single victory.

RACE	POINTS	YEARS
THE MONUMENTS – 3 POINTS EARNED		
MILAN–SAN REMO:	3	1991
WORLD CHAMPIONSHIP ROAD RACE - 2 POINTS EARNED		
SILVER	2	1994
CLASSICS/OLYMPICS/TIME TRIALS – 2 POINTS EARNED		
CLÁSICA DE SAN SEBASTIÁN	2	1993
SEMI-CLASSICS/NATIONALS – 4 POINTS EARNED		
TRE VALLE VARESINE	1	1994
GRAN PIEMONTE/GIRO DEL PIEMONTE	1	1989,1995
COPPA PLACCI	1	1989
MINOR TOURS AND STAGE RACES – 8 POINTS EARNED		
VOLTA A CATALUNYA/TOUR OF CATALONIA	3	1994
TOUR OF THE BASQUE COUNTRY/VUELTA CICLISTA AL PAIS VASCO	3	1991
TOUR OF THE ALPS/GIRO DEL TRENTINO	2	1992

ADDITIONAL CLAUDIO CHIAPPUCCI CONTINUED ON THE NEXT PAGE...

RACE	POINTS	YEARS
GRAND TOURS (VARIOUS POINTS) - 17 POINTS EARNED		
GIRO D'ITALIA		
2ND PLACE	3	1991, 1992
3RD PLACE	1	1993
TOUR DE FRANCE		
2ND PLACE	4	1990, 1992
3RD PLACE	2	1991
GRAND TOUR CLASSIFICATION JERSEYS - 12 POINTS EARNED		
GIRO D'ITALIA: POINTS	2	1991
GIRO D'ITALIA: MOUNTAINS	2	1990, 1992, 1993
TOUR DE FRANCE: MOUNTAINS	2	1991, 1992
GRAND TOUR STAGE WINS - 2.5 POINTS EARNED		
GIRO D'ITALIA: 1 STAGE	½ POINT	1987-1993
TOUR DE FRANCE: 3 STAGES	½ POINT	1991-1993
SEASON-LONG COMPETITIONS - 0 POINTS EARNED		
HOUR RECORD - 0 POINTS EARNED		
RACE RECORDS (VARIOUS POINTS) - 0 POINTS EARNED		
LIFETIME ACHIEVEMENTS (VARIOUS POINTS) - 0 POINTS EARNED		

Rank 45: Jan Ullrich

BORN: **DECEMBER 2, 1973**
YEARS ACTIVE: **1994–2006**
COUNTRY: **GERMANY**
NICKNAME:
DER KAISER (THE EMPEROR)

CAREER WINS: **31**
TOTAL POINTS: **50.5**
RAW SCORE: **50.5**

AFTER ERIK ZABEL, HE IS GERMANY'S TOP-RANKED RIDER, and he's also Germany's first Tour de France winner. Despite that victory in his sophomore appearance at the French Grand Tour in 1997, and his win the 1999 Vuelta, *Der Kaiser's* career is unfortunately best remembered by an "eternal second" label associated with his greatest rival, Lance Armstrong; Ullrich placed second to Armstrong in the Tour in 2000, 2001, and 2003, fourth in 2004, and third in 2005. That 2005 result was later removed from the record books for a doping violation by the Court of Arbitration for Sport, as was his single Giro stage victory in 2006 and his 2006 Tour of Switzerland overall victory. Ullrich was both a gifted climber and time trialist, and won the gold medal in the 2000 Summer Olympics RR, was twice world champion in the individual time trial (1999 and 2001), won the 2001 Giro dell'Emilia, and was twice Germany's national RR champion (1997 and 2001).

RACE	POINTS	YEARS
THE MONUMENTS – 0 POINTS EARNED		
WORLD CHAMPIONSHIP ROAD RACE - 0 POINTS EARNED		
CLASSICS/OLYMPICS/TIME TRIALS – 6 POINTS EARNED		
OLYMPIC ROAD RACE GOLD	2	2000
WORLD TT GOLD	2	1999, 2001
SEMI-CLASSICS/NATIONALS – 4 POINTS EARNED		
GERMAN NATIONAL RR CHAMPIONSHIPS	1	1997, 2001
EUROEYES CYCLASSICS/VATTENFALL CYCLASSICS, HEW CYCLASSICS	1	1997
GIRO DELL'EMILIA	1	2001
MINOR TOURS AND STAGE RACES – 3 POINTS EARNED		
TOUR OF SWITZERLAND/TOUR DE SUISSE	3	2004
GRAND TOURS (VARIOUS POINTS) - 33 POINTS EARNED		
TOUR DE FRANCE		
1ST PLACE	8	1997
2ND PLACE	4	1996, 1998, 2000, 2001, 2003
VUELTA A ESPAÑA (TOUR OF SPAIN)		
1ST PLACE (1974-PRESENT)	5	1999
GRAND TOUR CLASSIFICATION JERSEYS – 0 POINTS EARNED		
GRAND TOUR STAGE WINS – 4.5 POINTS EARNED		
TOUR DE FRANCE: 7 STAGES	½ POINT	1996-2003
VUELTA A ESPAÑA: 2 STAGES	½ POINT	1999
SEASON-LONG COMPETITIONS – 0 POINTS EARNED		
HOUR RECORD - 0 POINTS EARNED		
RACE RECORDS (VARIOUS POINTS) - 0 POINTS EARNED		
LIFETIME ACHIEVEMENTS (VARIOUS POINTS) – 0 POINTS EARNED		

Rank 46: Federico Bahamontes

BORN: **JULY 9, 1928**
YEARS ACTIVE: **1954–1965**
COUNTRY: **SPAIN**
NICKNAME: **THE EAGLE OF TOLEDO /
FEDE / BAHA**

CAREER WINS: **41**
TOTAL POINTS: **50.5**
RAW SCORE: **40.5**

BAHAMONTES IS ONE OF THE LEGENDARY CLIMBERS OF THE SPORT. Along with Gino Bartali, he is the only other cyclist to win nine mountains classifications in Grand Tours. Unlike Bartali, "The Eagle of Toledo" accomplished this feat by doing so in all three GTs; it is only he and the Colombian, Luis Herrera, who have managed to pull off this rare treble of King of the Mountains honors.

"Fede," known for his mercurial personality, often confounded the peloton with his strange behavior. During the 1956 Tour, he broke away at the foot of the first mountain in the Alps, the peloton giving furious chase only to find the Spaniard at the summit standing at the side of the road, casually eating an ice cream cone. Later he'd reveal that he had broken a spoke on the way up and was simply passing time while waiting for his team car to arrive. Whatever the reason for the bizarre incident, the story has become part of the legend and lore of the Tour de France. The following year in 1957, midway through the Tour, "Baha" inexplicably pulled to the side of the road and decided to call it quits, in his words, "Fede, he's not breathing well." As his team pleaded with him to continue, he took off his shoes and chucked them over the side of a ledge, his Tour officially over for that year.

Early in his career it sometimes seemed that Bahamontes took greater interest in winning the mountains classification rather than going for a high general classification placement in many of his stage race participations; he'd often attack at the first sight of a mountain with little regard given to how that might affect his overall chance of victory. That trend would change in the 1959 Tour de France, as the manager of his team that year was none other than the legendary Fausto Coppi. Baha rode a completely different race, riding at the front, participating in breakaways, and eschewing his typical blistering attacks at the arrival of the early mountain stages. Bahamontes would go on to win the 1959 Tour with a cushion of 4 minutes, 1 second over France's Henry Anglade, becoming Spain's first victor in the French Grand Tour. Tragically, Coppi succumbed to malaria in January 1960, and Fede was left without the guiding hand of one of the sport's all-time greats—he would not go on to win another Grand Tour. Although Coppi was gone, Bahamontes continued to pursue high GC placings, and he placed second in the Tour in 1963 and third in 1964, also collecting three straight mountains classifications in that same race from 1962 to 1964. A good case can be made that Federico Bahamontes was not only one of the best pure climbers the sport had ever witnessed, but perhaps *the* best.

ADDITIONAL FEDERICO BAHAMONTES CONTINUED ON THE NEXT PAGE...

RACE	POINTS	YEARS
THE MONUMENTS – 0 POINTS EARNED		
WORLD CHAMPIONSHIP ROAD RACE - 0 POINTS EARNED		
CLASSICS/OLYMPICS/TIME TRIALS – 0 POINTS EARNED		
SEMI-CLASSICS/NATIONALS – I POINT EARNED		
SPANISH NATIONAL RR CHAMPIONSHIPS	I	1958
MINOR TOURS AND STAGE RACES – 0 POINTS EARNED		
GRAND TOURS (VARIOUS POINTS) - 16 POINTS EARNED		
TOUR DE FRANCE		
IST PLACE	8	1959
2ND PLACE	4	1963
3RD PLACE	2	1964
VUELTA A ESPAÑA (TOUR OF SPAIN)		
2ND PLACE	2	1957
GRAND TOUR CLASSIFICATION JERSEYS – 18 POINTS EARNED		
GIRO D'ITALIA: MOUNTAINS	2	1956
TOUR DE FRANCE: MOUNTAINS	2	1954, 1958, 1959, 1962, 1963, 1964
VUELTA A ESPAÑA: MOUNTAINS	2	1957, 1958
GRAND TOUR STAGE WINS - 5.5 POINTS EARNED		
GIRO D'ITALIA: I STAGE	½ POINT	1958
TOUR DE FRANCE: 7 STAGES	½ POINT	1954-1965
VUELTA A ESPAÑA: 3 STAGES	½ POINT	1955-1965
SEASON-LONG COMPETITIONS – 0 POINTS EARNED		
HOUR RECORD - 0 POINTS EARNED		
RACE RECORDS (VARIOUS POINTS) – 0 POINTS EARNED		
LIFETIME ACHIEVEMENTS (VARIOUS POINTS) – 10 POINTS EARNED		
WON ANY EIGHT GRAND TOUR CLASSIFICATION JERSEYS: 10 POINTS		

Rank 47: Lucien Van Impe

BORN: **OCTOBER 20, 1946**
YEARS ACTIVE: **1969-1987**
COUNTRY: **BELGIUM**
NICKNAME: *DE KLEINE VAN MERE*
(THE LITTLE ONE FROM MERE)

CAREER WINS: **30**
TOTAL POINTS: **50**
RAW SCORE: **40**

VAN IMPE WAS ONE OF THE LEGENDARY CLIMBERS OF THE SPORT who, like both Charly Gaul and Federico Bahamontes, not only racked up numerous mountains classifications, but also actually won a Grand Tour. It might seem odd that a Belgian rider from the flatlands of Flanders was one of cycling's all-time great pure climbers, but his years of training in the hellish winds of the region must have been perfect preparation for the five-foot-six (1.68 meter) *grimpeur* to not only excel in the high mountains, but also hold his own in a time trial. "The Little One from Mere" not only won the 1976 Tour de France, but also finished second in 1981 and third in 1971, 1975, and 1977. He was King of the Mountains in the Tour de France six times, which in 1983 equaled the record of Bahamontes; he also captured the mountains classification in the Giro two times. Van Impe won eight Tour stages over his career and one each in both the Giro and Vuelta. Over the course of his remarkable eighteen years in the pro peloton, Van Impe completed a Grand Tour in every single one of them, except his last in 1987. What is even more remarkable is that he finished in the top ten in the general classification in fourteen of his twenty-one GT appearances. There is no doubt that Van Impe could have easily added more mountains classifications to his *palmarès* had he focused on those competitions rather than ride for a high GC placing. In deference to his childhood hero and mentor, he has stated that he intentionally chose not to break Federico Bahamontes's six King of the Mountain titles. As with both Bahamontes and Gaul, the case can certainly be made that Van Impe may have been the sport's greatest pure climber.

RACE	POINTS	YEARS
THE MONUMENTS – 0 POINTS EARNED		
WORLD CHAMPIONSHIP ROAD RACE – 0 POINTS EARNED		
CLASSICS/OLYMPICS/TIME TRIALS – 0 POINTS EARNED		
SEMI-CLASSICS/NATIONALS – 1 POINT EARNED		
BELGIAN NATIONAL RR CHAMPIONSHIPS	1	1983
MINOR TOURS AND STAGE RACES – 0 POINTS EARNED		
GRAND TOURS (VARIOUS POINTS) – 18 POINTS EARNED		
TOUR DE FRANCE		
1ST PLACE	8	1976
2ND PLACE	4	1981
3RD PLACE	2	1971, 1975, 1977
GRAND TOUR CLASSIFICATION JERSEYS – 16 POINTS EARNED		
GIRO D'ITALIA: MOUNTAINS	2	1982, 1983
TOUR DE FRANCE: MOUNTAINS	2	1971, 1972, 1975, 1977, 1981, 1983
GRAND TOUR STAGE WINS – 5 POINTS EARNED		
GIRO D'ITALIA: 1 STAGE	½ POINT	1983
TOUR DE FRANCE: 8 STAGES	½ POINT	1972-1983
VUELTA A ESPAÑA: 1 STAGE	½ POINT	1979

ADDITIONAL LUCIEN VAN IMPE CONTINUED ON THE NEXT PAGE...

SEASON-LONG COMPETITIONS – 0 POINTS EARNED

HOUR RECORD - 0 POINTS EARNED

RACE RECORDS (VARIOUS POINTS) – 0 POINTS EARNED

LIFETIME ACHIEVEMENTS (VARIOUS POINTS) – 10 POINTS EARNED

WON ANY EIGHT GRAND TOUR CLASSIFICATION JERSEYS: 10 POINTS

Rank 48: Stephen Roche

BORN: **NOVEMBER 28, 1959**
YEARS ACTIVE: **1981–1993**
COUNTRY: **IRELAND**
NICKNAME: **THE PAGE**

CAREER WINS: **52**
TOTAL POINTS: **49.5**
RAW SCORE: **49.5**

ASIDE FROM MERCKX, MAERTENS, JALABERT, AND COPPI, NOBODY HAS SCORED MORE POINTS IN A SINGLE SEASON THAN STEPHEN ROCHE. Over a remarkable six-month stretch in 1987, he captured the Tour of Romandy, the Giro d'Italia and three of its stages, the Tour de France and two of its stages, the World Championship Road Race, and also accumulated enough points along the way to secure the Super Prestige Pernod Trophy at the end of the season. It is only Merckx who has also won both Grand Tours and gold in the WC Road Race in the same year—cycling's Triple Crown. Roche earned a whopping 25.5 points in one year of racing. To put that into some context, that would have been only a single point shy of earning enough points to have made the Top 100 list. Conversely, without those points he wouldn't have ended up with nearly enough to have even made this list. That brilliant year has always been a bit of a puzzle. The Irishman turned pro in 1981 and prior to his breakout '87 season had won Paris-Nice in his rookie year, the Tour of Romandy in both 1983 and 1984, the Critérium International in 1985, and took third in the 1985 Tour de France. Those results were certainly no indication of what he would accomplish in his magical year, especially given that he suffered a horrible knee injury in 1986, didn't win a race that entire year, and finished in forty-eighth place in that summer's Tour de France. It is just so odd that he won so much the following year. His results after 1987 were fairly typical of his earlier successes—a win in the 1989 Tour of the Basque Country, the 1990 Four Days of Dunkirk, and the 1991 Critérium International and Setmana Catalana. His last points were scored by winning a stage in the 1992 Tour. After his knee injury flared up again in 1988, Roche was never again a factor in any GT; he had a total of eight starts from 1989 to 1993, with his highest placing a ninth in both the Giro and Tour.

RACE	POINTS	YEARS
THE MONUMENTS – 0 POINTS EARNED		
WORLD CHAMPIONSHIP ROAD RACE – 5 POINTS EARNED		
GOLD	4	1987
BRONZE	1	1983
CLASSICS/OLYMPICS/TIME TRIALS – 0 POINTS EARNED		
SEMI-CLASSICS/NATIONALS – 0 POINTS EARNED		
MINOR TOURS AND STAGE RACES – 23 POINTS EARNED		
PARIS-NICE	3	1981
TOUR OF THE BASQUE COUNTRY/VUELTA CICLISTA AL PAIS VASCO	3	1989
TOUR OF ROMANDY	3	1983, 1984, 1987
CRITÉRIUM INTERNATIONAL	2	1985, 1991
CATALAN WEEK/SETMANA CATALUNYA	2	1991
FOUR DAYS OF DUNKIRK	2	1990

ADDITIONAL STEPHEN ROCHE CONTINUED ON THE NEXT PAGE...

RACE	POINTS	YEARS
GRAND TOURS (VARIOUS POINTS) - 16 POINTS EARNED		
GIRO D'ITALIA		
1ST PLACE	6	1987
TOUR DE FRANCE		
1ST PLACE	8	1987
3RD PLACE	2	1985
GRAND TOUR CLASSIFICATION JERSEYS – 0 POINTS EARNED		
GRAND TOUR STAGE WINS - 3.5 POINTS EARNED		
GIRO D'ITALIA: 2 STAGES, 1 TTT	½ POINT	1987
TOUR DE FRANCE: 3 STAGES, 1 TTT	½ POINT	1985-1992
SEASON-LONG COMPETITIONS – 2 POINTS EARNED		
SUPER PRESTIGE PERNOD TROPHY	2	1987
HOUR RECORD - 0 POINTS EARNED		
RACE RECORDS (VARIOUS POINTS) – 0 POINTS EARNED		
LIFETIME ACHIEVEMENTS (VARIOUS POINTS) – 0 POINTS EARNED		

Rank 49: Alex Zulle

BORN: **JULY 5, 1968**
YEARS ACTIVE: **1991-2004**
COUNTRY: **SWITZERLAND**
NICKNAME: ***PERO LOCO* (CRAZY
DOG) / *ROMPETECHOS* (SPANISH
CARTOON CHARACTER WHO WORE
GLASSES)**

CAREER WINS: **65**
TOTAL POINTS: **48**
RAW SCORE: **48**

ZULLE WAS A SWISS STAGE RACE SPECIALIST WHOSE CAREER spanned
the Tour de France reigns of both Miguel Induráin and Lance
Armstrong. He was an excellent climber and talented time trialist.
His greatest successes were in Spain, which is no surprise given he
was part of the powerful Spanish Once squad from 1991 to 1997,
and he was also on Induráin's former team, Banesto, from 1999 to
2000. Zulle got his first taste of Grand Tour success by placing third
in the 1993 Vuelta, a race he would go on to win two years in a row
in 1996 and 1997. Zulle also won the Setmana Catalana in 1992 and
1996, the Tour of the Basque Country in 1995 and 1997, and the
Volta a Catalunya in 1996. His stage race victories weren't strictly
limited to Spain, as he did win Paris-Nice in 1993 and his home
country's Tour of Switzerland in 2002. His best chances of a GT win
outside of the Vuelta came in the Tour de France, when in 1995 he
finished second behind Miguel Induráin, and in 1999 when he again
finished in second place, this time behind Lance Armstrong. Zulle
is also remembered for being part of the infamous Festina squad
that was expelled from the 1998 Tour de France after their *soigner's*
vehicle was pulled over by customs officers, who discovered anabolic

steroids, EPO, syringes, and other doping products.* By the end of
2000, all nine members of the team had admitted to using EPO. The
Festina affair would unfortunately serve as only the first of several
high-profile doping investigations in the sport.

_____

*Of course a French term, a soigner is someone who looks after the cyclists—a
caretaker. They provide the daily massage, run errands, shuttle riders to and from
the airport, feed riders during the race, do laundry, and take care of first aid in the
absence of the doctors. They basically do everything except take care of the bikes._

RACE	POINTS	YEARS
THE MONUMENTS – 0 POINTS EARNED		
WORLD CHAMPIONSHIP ROAD RACE - 0 POINTS EARNED		
CLASSICS/OLYMPICS/TIME TRIALS – 2 POINTS EARNED		
WORLD TT GOLD	2	1996
SEMI-CLASSICS/NATIONALS – 0 POINTS EARNED		
MINOR TOURS AND STAGE RACES – 19 POINTS EARNED		
PARIS-NICE	3	1993
VOLTA A CATALUNYA/TOUR OF CATALONIA	3	1996
TOUR OF THE BASQUE COUNTRY/VUELTA CICLISTA AL PAIS VASCO	3	1995, 1997
TOUR OF SWITZERLAND/TOUR DE SUISSE	3	2002
CATALAN WEEK/SETMANA CATALUNYA	2	1992, 1996
GRAND TOURS (VARIOUS POINTS) - 20 POINTS EARNED		
TOUR DE FRANCE		
2ND PLACE	4	1995, 1999
VUELTA A ESPAÑA (TOUR OF SPAIN)		
1ST PLACE	5	1996, 1997
2ND PLACE	2	1993

ADDITIONAL ALEX ZULLE CONTINUED ON THE NEXT PAGE...

RACE	POINTS	YEARS
GRAND TOUR CLASSIFICATION JERSEYS – 0 POINTS EARNED		
GRAND TOUR STAGE WINS - 7 POINTS EARNED		
GIRO D'ITALIA: 3 STAGES	½ POINT	1998
TOUR DE FRANCE: 2 STAGES	½ POINT	1995-1996
VUELTA A ESPAÑA: 9 STAGES	½ POINT	1993-2000
SEASON-LONG COMPETITIONS – 0 POINTS EARNED		
HOUR RECORD - 0 POINTS EARNED		
RACE RECORDS (VARIOUS POINTS) – 0 POINTS EARNED		
LIFETIME ACHIEVEMENTS (VARIOUS POINTS) – 0 POINTS EARNED		

Rank 50: Hugo Koblet

BORN: **MARCH 21, 1925**
YEARS ACTIVE: **1946-1958**
COUNTRY: **SWITZERLAND**
NICKNAME: *LE PEDALEUR DU*
CHARME (THE PEDALER OF CHARM)
/ BEAUTIFUL HUGO

CAREER WINS: **55**
TOTAL POINTS: **48**
RAW SCORE: **48**

Koblet is one of pro cycling's great mysteries, a cyclist rising from almost complete anonymity to dominate two Grand Tours in 1950 and 1951, and then strangely fading just as he'd reached the top rung of the ladder. He was almost unknown when he lined up for the 1950 Giro. Sure, he'd been the Swiss national track pursuit champion for four years running, finished third in the Worlds in that same event in 1947, and had also won a couple of stages in both the Tour of Romandy and Tour of Switzerland. He'd even won a couple of big six-day races in the United States, but there was absolutely no reason to think the handsome and charming Swiss rider was capable of winning a Grand Tour. Yet, not only did he win that 1950 Giro, but he took two of the stages, captured the mountains classification, and defeated a living legend in Gino Bartali (Fiorenzo Magni and Ferdi Kübler were also in the race). Koblet became the first non-Italian to win the event in its thirty-two-year history. His next win would be in that summer's Tour of Switzerland, and Koblet was now a superstar—he would certainly be a marked man in future Grand Tours.

He had a quiet start to the 1951 season, and although he did compete in the Giro against another stacked field, Koblet was not able to defend his title, finishing over six minutes down on Magni in sixth place. He'd obviously been saving himself for the Tour de France, and when that race started, he was immediately on the attack, forcing the peloton to chase him down after only 40 kilometers had been covered on the first stage. The field that year included a veritable who's who of legendary cyclists, including Fausto Coppi, Gino Bartali, Fiorenzo Magni, Louison Bobet, Jean Robic, Raphaël Géminiani, and Stan Ockers.* After winning the stage seven time trial, it was obvious Koblet was in superb shape, and he drove that point home four stages later with one of the greatest Tour performances in history. The Swiss rider broke away on stage eleven after only 37 kilometers (23 miles) had been covered. The pack thought it a suicidal attack with 140 rolling kilometers (92 miles) still to go, but when the gap widened out to over three minutes, they were forced to chase. After the domestiques were unable to close on Koblet, the team leaders were forced to take over, but they too were unable to bridge gap. As Koblet crossed the finish line, he sat up and dabbed his face with a sponge stowed in his jersey pocket, then retrieved a comb and nonchalantly slicked back his hair. Thus was born the nickname that would stick with him for the rest of his career—"The Pedaler of Charm." The peloton, led by some of finest cyclists in history, crossed the line 3 minutes, 35 seconds later. Even after that epic break, Koblet was not yet in yellow, but that changed when the race entered the Pyrenees. By the time the race had exited the mountains, he held a lead of over nine minutes and had won two more stages. The stage twenty-two time trial was a mere formality, yet once again, Koblet crushed the competition

---

*Coppi was not at his best in that Tour, grief stricken over the recent death of his brother, Serse, who had unexpectedly succumbed to a head injury sustained in the Giro del Piemonte, just six days before the start of the Tour.

ADDITIONAL HUGO KOBLET CONTINUED ON THE NEXT PAGE...

and wound up winning that 1951 Tour by an incredible twenty-two-minute margin. It would be the last time the dashing Swiss rider would win a Grand Tour or even complete the Tour de France.

After the 1951 season concluded, Koblet went to Mexico; he had been invited to follow the country's national amateur tour. He returned a changed man. No one knows exactly what happened on that trip, but he must have contracted some type of illness or malady, and he was never again the same cyclist. He still possessed the same beautiful, flowing pedaling style, what the French call *souplesse*, but he was no longer able to generate the same power. His sole victory in the 1952 season was his home country's Zuri-Metzgete single-day race. Koblet won the 1953 Tour of Romandy and then finished a close second to Coppi in that year's Giro, which would be the closest he'd ever get to another GT victory. As photographs from the mid-1950s reveal, he was in a rapid decline—it seemed as though the handsome *Pedaleur du Charme* had aged ten or more years in the span of a few seasons (his bio photo on page 272 is circa 1952-1954, and the photo below is from 1956). His last victory was a stage

in the 1955 Vuelta, and he hung up his cleats in 1958. Six years after his retirement, he had a high-speed collision in his Alfa Romeo, driving head-on into a tree. He died four days later from his injuries. Witnesses claimed that he'd passed the tree twice, turning around each time before finally hitting it on the third pass. It's likely he committed suicide, but it's another one of the great mysteries in the life of Hugo Koblet that will go unsolved.

RACE	POINTS	YEARS
THE MONUMENTS – 0 POINTS EARNED		
WORLD CHAMPIONSHIP ROAD RACE - 0 POINTS EARNED		
CLASSICS/OLYMPICS/TIME TRIALS – 6 POINTS EARNED		
CHAMPIONSHIP OF ZURICH/ZURI-METZGETE	2	1952, 1954
GRAND PRIX DE NATIONS	2	1951
SEMI-CLASSICS/NATIONALS – 2 POINTS EARNED		
SWISS NATIONAL RR CHAMPIONSHIPS	1	1955
CRITÉRIUM DES AS	1	1951
MINOR TOURS AND STAGE RACES – 12 POINTS EARNED		
TOUR OF ROMANDY	3	1953
TOUR OF SWITZERLAND/TOUR DE SUISSE	3	1950, 1953, 1955
GRAND TOURS (VARIOUS POINTS) - 20 POINTS EARNED		
GIRO D'ITALIA		
1ST PLACE	6	1950
2ND PLACE	3	1953, 1954
TOUR DE FRANCE		
1ST PLACE	8	1951
GRAND TOUR CLASSIFICATION JERSEYS – 2 POINTS EARNED		
GIRO D'ITALIA: MOUNTAINS	2	1950
GRAND TOUR STAGE WINS - 6 POINTS EARNED		
GIRO D'ITALIA: 6 STAGES	½ POINT	1950-1955
TOUR DE FRANCE: 5 STAGES	½ POINT	1951
VUELTA A ESPAÑA: 1 STAGE	½ POINT	1956
SEASON-LONG COMPETITIONS – 0 POINTS EARNED		
HOUR RECORD - 0 POINTS EARNED		
RACE RECORDS (VARIOUS POINTS) – 0 POINTS EARNED		
LIFETIME ACHIEVEMENTS (VARIOUS POINTS) – 0 POINTS EARNED		

Epilogue

PELOTON LEGENDS

Errors

Every effort has been made to make sure the statistics used in this book are accurate. I'm sure there will be errors that I've missed, but please keep in mind that this is a self-published book and all the costs in bringing it to life were incurred by yours truly; these included design and formatting, photo rights, editing, and printing. Unfortunately, part of those expenditures did not include the budget to be able to hire a professional statistician to fact check all the thousands of numbers used within these covers.

Female Cyclists

Where are the women? The simple answer is that based on the framework of the scoring system used to rank cyclists, there was absolutely no possible way to include female cyclists as part of *Peloton Legends*. If you go back and revisit *Part 3: Scoring*, you'll see that the most significant feature of the races included are that

Marianne Vos

they have existed for at least 40 years. Unfortunately, the women's professional peloton simply doesn't yet have the longevity necessary to meet that particular benchmark. Aside from the World Championship Road Race, the current UCI Women's World Tour calendar only includes one race with a 40-year history, which is the Trofeo Alfredo Binda-Comune di Cittiglio, around since 1974. Certainly, one of the things that needs to happen for the women's side of the sport to grow and gain in popularity, and attract more sponsorship money, is stability to the racing calendar; the same races need to remain in place from one year to the next. I'm hoping that the UCI can provide the leadership needed to grow the women's side of professional road cycling so that *Peloton Legends* can one day also include cyclists such as Marianne Vos.

Updates

Peloton Legends is a work in progress. As I type these words, the 2020 season is underway and by the time some of you have read this there may have already been some changes to certain rider's point totals, perhaps even their ranking. Each year that passes, this book will obviously be a less relevant snapshot of the Top 100 Cyclists of the Modern Era. As mentioned in the preface, this ranking system once resided on my website, The Virtual Musette, and will once again find its permanent home back on another website - PelotonLegends.com. As of early 2020 that site has yet to launch, but it is where you will be able to eventually find updates to this project.

What does the future hold?

As this book goes to press the Covid-19 pandemic is raging around the world, and exactly how many races will actually take place during the 2020 season is unknown. Some of what I've written about below might not be addressed until the 2021 season.

I'm excited about the current crop of young riders who seem to have exploded on the scene the past couple of years. I'm guessing that some of the names we'll see in the Top 50 in another 10 years, or even sooner, will include Egan Bernal, Remco Evenepoel, Mathieu van der Poel, and Tadej Pogačar. They are all ridiculously talented, have already notched huge wins, and seem eager to etch their names in the history books. It should be fun watching these guys over the years, especially Bernal. Sure, he's a stage race specialist, but he struck me as much more than a one trick pony in 2019 with his success and aggression during his late season Italian single-day racing campaign, capped by his win in the Gran Piemonte.

Primož Roglič is not a young man, but he has only been a cyclist for eight years; not a pro cyclist mind you, but a cyclist who only took up the sport in 2012 in his early 20s. He cracked the Top 100 in 2019 and seems to be getting better each year. The case can be made that he's not that much more experienced than of some of those young guns listed above; he only received his first opportunity as a Grand Tour team leader in the 2019 Giro. I look at him more like 25-year-old, rather than someone who is actually 30. He's obviously a threat in any stage race he enters, but based on his wins in the Giro dell'Emilia and Tre Valli Veresine in 2019, I can't help but think he's going to capture Lombardia or any one of the Ardennes Classics at some point. We may be witnessing one of the great all-rounders in the sport who's still in the early stages of his career. He had a massive 19.5-point-year in 2019, which is right up there with some of best ever. To put that into perspective, if he has another few seasons like that, he'll be in the Top 20.

It will be interesting to see if Chris Froome can make it back to the same level of fitness he had before his horrible accident in the summer of 2019. He seems incredibly determined, but I just don't see it happening in 2020. He can make the Top 10 by the end of his career, but it will take another Grand Tour victory to do so. Finishing second or third on the podium, even multiple times, is not going to garner him enough points to overhaul the current number 10 on the list, Alejandro Valverde, who is still riding and winning.

When will Peter Sagan finally win Milan-San Remo? I would be amazed if he doesn't bag at least one victory in this race. He's started the race nine times, finished every one of them with his lowest placing being 17th, and he's finished in 2nd place twice. He seems destined to come out on top one of these days. Also, is "Peto" going to capture his eighth points classification jersey in the 2020 Giro or Tour? It's not really a matter of if he'll capture another one of these competitions, but when and where. When he does add another one of these contests to his *palmarès*, he'll receive a huge 10-point lifetime bonus for the achievement and crack the Top 25.

Will Tom Dumoulin get back to his best and again become a Grand Tour threat? He seemed to be on the fast track to break into the Top 100; his knee injury in the 2019 Giro seemed like no big deal, but it turned out to be much more severe and he missed the rest of the season. It's interesting that there's absolutely nothing on his Wiki page about the injury, but his new team says he is completely recovered and will have no ill effects from the injury. He's now on the same Jumbo-Visma team with Roglič, so even if he is back to 100%, there's no guarantee he'll even be the leader on his own team should the two start the same races. I guess they'll figure out who's the strongest during the race, ala Team Ineos.

Will Philippe Gilbert join cycling immortals Rik Van Looy, Eddy
Merckx, and Roger De Vlaeminck by winning Milan-San Remo
joining them as victors of all five Monuments? I think it's quite a
long shot. Gilbert has competed in the race 15 times and has
finished every one of them. He has come close by placing third
twice, but that last podium was all the way back in 2011. In his last
four starts, his highest placing was 29th. I think his best shot at
winning this race will be to launch from afar, sometime before the
final two climbs. If he waits for the final sprint, I just don't think
he's got the speed needed to hold off the fast men. Should he
manage the rare feat, he'd receive a huge 15-point lifetime bonus,
and would slot in right behind Mario Cipollini and occupy the 28th
spot on this list, just ahead of Raymond Poulidor. Gilbert signed a
three-year contract with Lotto-Soudal starting in 2020, so he
probably has only three chances left at capturing *La Classicissima di
Primavera* (The Spring Classic).

Will Nairo Quintana ever be a factor in another Grand Tour? His last
podium was a 2nd place in the 2017 Giro. Since then he's finished
12th in the 2017 Tour, 10th in the 2018 Tour, 8th in the 2018 Vuelta,
8th in the 2019 Tour, and 4th in the 2019 Vuelta. Maybe his move
away from the Movistar team to the Arkéa-Samsic squad will
rejuvenate his career.

Can Mark Cavendish find his way back to the top step of the podium
or is his career effectively over? I touched on this in back in the last
section in the Scoring Sheets, but he only needs a single victory in
any race during the entire season to receive a huge 10-point bonus
and jump up 10 places in the rankings. Again, like Quintana, just
maybe the switch he's made to a new team this year will provide the
spark to jump start whatever is needed to reverse his tail spin.

The Big Question

Will anyone ever get to 150 points in this scoring system again? Sean Kelly was the last to do so and that was over 30 years ago. Rik Van Looy, who is in 9th place, is the closest to that 150-point benchmark with a total of 152 points. In 2019 Alejandro Valverde made the jump into the 10th spot with 115 points. That's a huge 37-point gap between 9th and 10th places. To add some context to that difference, 37 points are enough to slot into 66th place on this list; it's basically an entire career's worth of points. It is mind boggling that there can be that much difference in scoring between cyclists who are only separated by one place in these rankings. Those top nine cyclists are who I consider to be cycling's royalty - the best of the best. I wonder how long it will take before anyone can add their names to following list of peloton legends?

- Eddy Merckx
- Bernard Hinault
- Fausto Coppi
- Gino Bartali
- Jacques Anquetil
- Sean Kelly
- Francesco Moser
- Roger De Vlaeminck
- Rik Van Looy

Changes to the Rankings

If you want to stay up to date on changes to the rankings, please visit PelotonLegends.com and subscribe to the *Peloton Legends* newsletter. There is also a blog at the site where there will be articles and updates, and over time, the career highlights and scoring sheets for the other 50 cyclists not in this book will also be featured. If you want to learn more about the author, how to contact him, or purchase branded merchandise, all that can also be found at the website.

Image Credits

PELOTON LEGENDS

Rachel Petruccillo/Etsy store CyclingArtStudio (Illustrations)

Part 1, Gino Bartali
Part 2, Fausto Coppi
Part 3, Jacques Anquetil
Part 4, Eddy Merckx
Part 5, Bernard Hinault
Page 75, Fiorenzo Magni
Page 286, "La Trouée", Eddy Merckx

Cor Vos

Front Cover, Hugo Koblet and Fausto Coppi
Preface, Page VII, Miguel Indurain
Preface, Page VIII, Roger De Vlaeminck
Page 7, Erik Zabel
Page 9, Marco Pantani
Page 9, Nairo Quintana
Page 23, Illustration of Fausto Coppi
Page 25, Illustration of Gino Bartali
Page 27, Illustration of Bartali, Coppi, Magni – Cor Vos and Cartoonist Nesten
Page 28, Bernard Hinault
Page 32, Louison Bobet
Page 32, Laurent Fignon
Page 33, Greg LeMond
Page 53, Jan Janssen
Page 54, Felice Gimondi
Page 68, Charly Mottet
Page 69, Luis Herrera
Page 71, Andy Hampsten
Page 71, Edwig Van Hooydonck
Page 96, Gino Bartali
Page 103, Jacques Anquetil
Page 104, Sean Kelly
Page 107, Sean Kelly
Page 111, Francesco Moser
Page 112, Roger De Vlaeminck
Page 119, Rik Van Looy
Page 124, Miguel Induráin
Page 128, Felice Gimondi
Page 139, Laurent Jalabert
Page 155, Tony Rominger
Page 160, Giuseppe Saronni
Page 163, Giuseppe Sarroni
Page 171, Joop Zoetemelk
Page 187, Rik Van Steenbergen
Page 191, Mario Cipollini
Page 196, Johan Museeuw
Page 199, Johan Museeuw
Page 200, Greg LeMond

Page 203, Greg LeMond
Page 208, Jan Janssen
Page 212, Laurent Fignon
Page 215, Laurent Fignon
Page 219, Luis Ocaña
Page 223, Paolo Bettini
Page 230, Franco Bitossi
Page 249, Moreno Argentin
Page 253, Claudio Chiappucci
Page 260, Lucien Van Impe
Page 263, Lucien Van Impe
Page 264, Stephen Roche
Page 267, Stephen Roche
Page 271, Alex Zulle
Page 277, Marianne Vos
Back Cover, Jan Raas

Alamy

Page 3, Philippe Thys
Page 5, Lucien "Petit-Breton"
Page 12, Gino Bartali
Page 13, Learco Guerra
Page 16, Roger Lapébie
Page 17, Nicolas Frantz
Page 24, Gino Bartali
Page 29, Miguel Induráin
Page 31, Eddy Merckx
Page 52, Eddy Merckx
Page 57, Rik Van Steenbergen
Page 82, Eddy Merckx
Page 95, Fausto Coppi
Page 99, Gino Bartali
Page 144, Chris Froome
Page 151, Ferdi Kübler
Page 157, Fiorenzo Magni
Page 164, Alberto Contador
Page 176, Erik Zabel
Page 179, Erik Zabel
Page 195, Raymond Poulidor
Page 211, Jan Janssen
Page 216, Luis Ocaña
Page 220, Paolo Bettini
Page 236, Gianni Bugno
Page 243, Philippe Gilbert
Page 246, Moreno Argentin
Page 250, Claudio Chiappucci
Page 254, Jan Ullrich
Page 259, Federico Bahamontes
Page 272, Hugo Koblet

Wikimedia Commons

Page 4, Ottavio Bottecchia, Bibliothèque Nationale de France
Page 5, Lucien Buysse, Public Domain
Page 7, Henri Péllisier, Public Domain
Page 8, Henri Desgrange, Bibliothèque Nationale de France
Comparing Cycling's Two Major Eras, Page II, Alfredo Binda, Mondonico Collection
Page 15, Oscar Egg, United States Library of Congress
Page 16, Super Champion Osgear, Creative Commons of Nicola
Page 87, Eddy Merckx, Dutch National Archives
Page 88, Bernard Hinault, Dutch National Archives
Page 92, Fausto Coppi, Dutch National Archives
Page 100, Jacques Anquetil, Dutch National Archives
Page 108, Francesco Moser, Dutch National Archives
Page 116, Rik Van Looy, Dutch National Archives
Page 120, Alejandro Valverde, Wiki author Granada
Page 127, Miguel Induráin, Wiki author Eric Houdas
Page 132, Louison Bobet, Dutch National Archives
Page 136, Laurent Jalabert, Wiki author Eric Houdas
Page 140, Freddy Maertens, Dutch National Archives
Page 147, Chris Froome, Wiki author Gyrostat
Page 148, Ferdi Kübler, Dutch National Archive
Page 152, Tony Rominger, Wiki author Eric Houdas
Page 167, Alberto Contador, Wiki author Filip Bossuyt
Page 168, Joop Zoetemelk, Dutch National Archives
Page 172, Vincenzo Nibali, Wiki author Carlos Delgado
Page 175, Vincenzo Nibali, Wiki author Sanguinez
Page 180, Tom Boonen, Wiki author Jérémy-Günther-Heinz Jähnick
Page 183, Tom Boonen, Wiki author Roxanne King
Page 184, Rik Van Steenbergen, Dutch National Archives
Page 188, Mario Cipollini, Wiki author Eric Houdas
Page 192, Raymond Poulidor, Dutch National Archives
Page 204, Peter Sagan, Wiki author Jérémy-Günther-Heinz Jähnick
Page 207, Peter Sagan, Wiki author Filip Bossuyt
Page 224, Fabian Cancellara, Flickr account of Tim Moreillon
Page 226, Charly Gaul, Dutch National Archive
Page 234, Mark Cavendish, Wiki author Antoine Blondin
Page 240, Philippe Gilbert, Flickr account of s.yuki
Page 244, Jan Raas, Dutch National Archives
Page 256, Federico Bahamontes, Dutch National Archives
Page 268, Alex Zulle, wiki author Eric Houdas
Page 274, Hugo Koblet, Dutch National Archives

Rustyshutters Etsy Shop

Page 21, Fausto Coppi Crash

Acknowledgements

This project would have never been possible without the amazing work and efforts of other cycling historians who have shared their work online. Thank you to all the following:

Tom James, both VeloArchive and Professional Cycling Palmares
WWW.VELOARCHIVE.COM (DEFUNCT)

Bill and Carol McGann, Bike Race Info
WWW.BIKERACEINFO.COM

Sam Barrows, Cycling Hall of Fame
WWW.CYCLINGHALLOFFAME.COM (DEFUNCT)

Barry Boyce and Graham Jones, Cycling Revealed
WWW.CYCLINGREVEALED.COM

Stephan van der Zwan at ProCyclingStats
WWW.PROCYCLINGSTATS.COM

Andy Roose, Jasper van Hoof,
and the rest of the team at Cycling Quotient
WWW.CQRANKING.COM

The team at Velopalmares (French)
WWW.VELOPALMARES.FREE.FR

The team at Memoire du cyclisme (French)
WWW.MEMOIRE-DU-CYCLISME.EU

Printed in Great Britain
by Amazon